Surveying Immigrant Communities

Policy Imperatives and Technical Challenges

Julie DaVanzo
Jennifer Hawes-Dawson
R. Burciaga Valdez
Georges Vernez

with Christina Andrews, Barbara Levitan,
Joyce E. Peterson, Robert F. Schoeni

Supported by
The Ford Foundation

RAND

In its 1985 report *Immigration Statistics: A Story of Neglect*, the National Research Council concluded that the current immigration information system could never produce reliable, accurate, and timely statistics that permit rational decisionmaking about immigration policy. Mere patching of ongoing data collection systems would not solve the problem. The Council recommended that Congress make "profound and basic" changes, including the funding and implementation of a dedicated new data collection effort focusing on new immigrants over a five-year period, in order to "develop information for policy guidance on the adjustment experience of families and individuals to the labor market, use of educational and health facilities, reliance on social programs, mobility experience, and income history."

This recommendation was never acted upon. And today, Congress, state, and local policymakers still have no reliable answers to basic questions about the costs and benefits of immigration for state and local governments, for the economy as a whole, and for the nature and speed of integration of new immigrants into U.S. society.

A lack of confidence about feasibility and concerns about the costs of a dedicated survey of new immigrants are two of the many reasons why such an effort has not been undertaken. Can a representative sample of immigrants be drawn? How many groups of immigrants need to be included? What unique obstacles would such a survey encounter? Can we afford it? To address these questions, the RAND Center for Research on Immigration Policy undertook a pilot survey of Salvadoran and Filipino immigrants in Los Angeles, the results of which are presented in this report.

We conclude that conducting a national survey of immigrants is feasible, although expensive, and can provide reliable answers to critical immigration policy questions, including the issue of undocumented immigration. Surely such an effort would present unique challenges in personnel recruitment, multilingual questionnaire development, and field monitoring. But at every level, the public debate on immigration *does* need the new data that a specially designed national survey can provide.

The project was funded by the Ford Foundation and by the Center for Research on Immigration Policy. The latter, created in February 1988, first focused on assessing the implementation and effects of the Immigration Reform and Control Act of 1986. It then began to study the larger, continuing questions of integration of immigrants into the economic, social, and political life of the receiving country and to assess the demands immigrants are placing on its institutions, including schools, postsecondary educational institutions, and local governments. The center also has examined the link between immigration and key foreign and international policy issues associated with a potential North American economic integration and with the fundamental changes brought about by European integration and the liberalization and restructuring in Eastern Europe and the former Soviet Union.

The center also disseminates and exchanges information concerning immigration and immigrant policies. Researchers interested in receiving publications or in attending working groups and conferences should address inquiries to:

Georges Vernez
Director, Center for Research on Immigration Policy
RAND
1700 Main Street
P.O. Box 2138
Santa Monica, CA 90407

CONTENTS

Appendix

FIGURES

Immigration to the United States poses major challenges to society—and it is clearly a force on the rise. As the nation debates how immigrants affect society and the economy and how best to absorb them, participants at every level need more information about immigrants and how they affect the national life. Current data sources simply do not provide the range and kinds of information they need.

Researchers and policymakers cannot rely on case studies, convenience-sample surveys, and indirect estimates. They need entirely new data. To provide the statistical confidence necessary for important policy decisions, the new data must come from a large number of immigrants. To shed light on the diverse populations now entering the United States, the data must be drawn from several different ethnic and regional groups. And to describe the complex, long-term process of immigrant adaptation—which almost certainly involves major changes in social-service needs and economic contributions—the data should cover several points over time. Only data like these can finally provide reliable guidance for policy that covers the flow of immigrants, the nature and needs of immigrants themselves, and their effects on society.

The most effective way of collecting such data would be a new national survey of immigrants. However, some have argued that a large-scale survey of immigrants—particularly one aimed at describing changes over time—may not be feasible. It is likely to be difficult and expensive and raises many challenges in design and implementation: for example, identifying immigrant households, overcoming language barriers, and getting adequate response rates.

To see whether such problems can, in fact, be overcome, we undertook a pilot study: the Los Angeles Community Survey (LACS) of Salvadorans and Filipinos, conducted in 1991. This report describes in detail the nature and results of that survey. This summary focuses more on the implications and recommendations for future surveys.

A BRIEF DESCRIPTION OF THE LACS

Our pilot effort faced many of the same challenges, albeit on a smaller scale, that a national survey would confront: deciding which immigrant populations to survey, recruiting and training bilingual staff, identifying neighborhoods where populations of interest are concentrated, developing and testing culturally appropriate survey

- Finding enough qualified interviewer applicants, particularly if special skills/ characteristics, such as bilingualism, are needed.

- Finding local residents who are willing to work as interviewers in high-crime inner cities.

- Keeping interviewers motivated to complete their assignments.

- Mounting effective community outreach activities to solicit support for the survey from community leaders and local residents.

- Designing effective training programs for complicated questionnaires and complex field procedures.

- Hiring a sufficient number of experienced supervisors.

- Implementing appropriate quality control checks, especially for new staff, throughout the fieldwork to gauge interviewer performance and data quality.

Despite the similarities, immigrant surveys have unique aspects that make the data collection management tasks (recruitment, training, supervision, and quality control) considerably more complicated and time-consuming to implement successfully. Many of these aspects are related to cultural and linguistic differences.

Recommendations for Survey Procedures

The pilot survey revealed several critical research issues that must be addressed to ensure the success of future surveys of immigrant populations.

1. Identifying a sample of immigrants. There is a serious potential pitfall in the sampling process that must be avoided to ensure the success of sampling procedures. It is crucial to list and screen all addresses in target areas, especially many hidden apartment units that may not be easily visible from the street and are likely to house one or more immigrant families. The failure to properly list addresses for immigrant samples can lead to a serious undercount of immigrants, especially those who are undocumented.

To minimize these listing problems, future surveys should

- Use a team of bilingual field interviewers, who are comfortable working in the target areas, to complete both the listing activities and the actual screening and interviewing.

- Validate a random percentage of each lister's work to ensure the accuracy of the listings before the actual fieldwork begins.

- Provide adequate training for interviewers on field listing so that they can identify potential listing problems when they are in the field.

2. Developing and testing questionnaires suitable for administration with different immigrant groups. The design and testing of effective instruments in several languages is time-consuming and requires close collaboration between the design team, the translators, and outside consultants.

- The designers should consider translatability of measures during the early stages of instrument design, so that the English and non-English questionnaires are developed in parallel.

- The survey should hire highly skilled translators who are familiar with the study population(s) and the spoken language they use, and have some familiarity with survey research, to work closely with the survey team during the design and testing process and during the preparation of the final version of all survey materials.

- All survey instruments should be pretested extensively in all languages with respondents from the target groups, using multiple pretesting methods, as appropriate.

- Bilingual interviewers who are representative of the immigrant populations that will be included in the study should conduct the testing of translated instruments.

- Bilingual members of the survey design team should attend some of the pretest interviews to observe the interviewer-respondent interactions as the translated instruments are being tested in the field.

A random percentage of test interviews should be observed by a bilingual field supervisor (this step could be incorporated into field validation) to monitor respondent reaction to the translated instruments. It would also be useful to collect systematic data from interviewers about their perceptions of how well the translated instruments really worked. Results from both these steps would improve researchers' understanding of whether the translated instruments meet the design objective.

3. Recruiting and retaining a high-quality bilingual field staff. Without a highly skilled and committed bilingual field interviewing staff, surveys of immigrant populations whose first language is not English cannot be successfully implemented. The LACS staff's performance exceeded our expectations and is largely responsible for the survey's success. Our ability to successfully recruit and retain a large bilingual staff throughout the field period rested on four key elements:

- We identified a qualified pool of bilingual interviewers from the same immigrant groups that were included in the study.

- We conducted extensive training sessions on the background and purpose of the study, aggressively solicited feedback from interviewers about their concerns, and gave them an opportunity to ask questions until they were comfortable with the project and their role as interviewers.

- The interviewers saw themselves as members of the research team and were dedicated to making the project a success. They were convinced that the survey might have a future positive effect on the Salvadoran and Filipino communities.

ACKNOWLEDGMENTS

We are indebted to the hundreds of Salvadoran and Filipino immigrants whom we interviewed. They were generous with their time and enthusiastic about their participation in this survey.

A number of other individuals made important contributions to the early development and conduct of the Los Angeles Community Survey. Julie Brown and Audrey Burnam helped with the early stages of development of the survey instruments. Ellen Kraly, Barry Edmonston, Jeffrey S. Passel, and Robert Gardiner provided useful comments on an early version of questionnaires.

The study was conducted by several researchers and truly represents an interdisciplinary effort. Julie DaVanzo and Robert Burciaga Valdez planned and directed the day-to-day operations of the overall effort and, with the assistance of Christina Andrews, were primarily responsible for the analysis presented in Chapter Four. Jennifer Hawes-Dawson and Barbara Levitan coordinated the fieldwork and were responsible for writing Chapter Three. Georges Vernez conceived the project, oversaw the overall effort, and wrote the analysis in Chapter Five. Robert Schoeni performed the multivariate analyses reported in that chapter.

Many others at RAND made significant contributions. Allan Abrahamse designed the sampling strategy for the LACS and drew the sample, with assistance from Laural Hill. Beverly Weidmer assisted with questionnaire design and the translation of survey materials into Spanish, and supervised the Spanish-speaking field interviewers. Donna Hill-Schwichtenberg supervised the field staff who interviewed the Filipino sample. They, along with Eve Fielder and Judy Perlman, provided valuable assistance during the training of interviewers and the preparation of training materials. Sandra Berry provided helpful advice on many different aspects of the project throughout its duration. Gary Bjork provided guidance regarding the structure of this report and the coordination across different chapters.

Theo Downes-LeGuin and Elizabeth Rolph reviewed and commented on the draft of the final report and provided many helpful comments.

We also wish to thank Joyce Peterson, who took a lengthy draft report, reorganized it, and helped communicate the study's findings directly. Finally we appreciate the careful editing of Nikki Shacklett and the excellent secretarial assistance provided by Pat Williams, Gloria Gowan, and Kevin Mason.

PURPOSES AND STRUCTURE OF THE REPORT

The purposes of this report are threefold: (1) to address key methodological issues in conducting a large-scale immigrant survey by describing the design, implementation, and field results of the LACS; (2) to demonstrate that such a survey can supply data needed to guide immigration and immigrant policy; and (3) to point out lessons learned from the LACS that can inform design and implementation of a national survey. To these ends, the report is structured as follows:

In Chapter Two, we discuss the issues facing policymakers and the reasons why a new data-collection effort is imperative to address those issues.

Chapter Three describes the LACS and how we approached design and implementation challenges for a large-scale immigrant survey: For example, what are the unique survey design and operational issues that must be considered in planning immigrant surveys? Can a large, bilingual field interviewing staff be successfully recruited, trained, and supervised? How much effort is involved in selecting an area probability sample of different immigrant groups?

Chapter Four reports on the experiences and field results of the survey and how they answer other questions critical for considering the feasibility of a national immigrant survey: What kinds of household screening procedures work? What kinds of participation and response rates can be expected from immigrants? Can complete and reliable data be collected from immigrants, especially sensitive information about their legal status and tracking data for possible follow-ups over time?

In Chapter Five, we describe survey results in the context of policy questions that the data allow policymakers to explore. This exercise demonstrates how important it is to distinguish among immigrant groups in formulating immigrant policies, since different groups have different needs and present different policy challenges.

Chapter Six summarizes both our methodological and substantive conclusions and discusses what we have learned that can provide guidance for a future national immigrant survey.

Chapter Two

POLICY CONTEXT AND DATA NEEDS FOR ASSESSING THE EFFECTS OF IMMIGRATION

Although the United States has an explicit immigration policy, it has rarely explicitly addressed issues of *immigrant* policy, such as housing, language, educational, and other assistance programs designed to help immigrants become full, participating members of the community. For example, recent changes in immigration laws, including the Immigration Reform and Control Act (IRCA) of 1986 and the 1990 immigration quota changes, have focused on changing or modifying the flow of people into the United States. As a nation, however, we are increasingly ambivalent about the nature and level of direct assistance that these immigrants should receive to facilitate their adjustment to life in the United States.

Other countries (e.g., Canada, Israel, and France) with high immigration rates have explicit policies and programs to help immigrants adjust to life in their new countries (U.S. GAO, 1992). But few data are currently available to answer the many questions relevant for assessing whether the United States should develop explicit immigrant policies, much less what such policies would be. In this chapter we discuss the policy issues briefly, what questions must be answered, and why current data sources are unequal to the task.

THE CHALLENGES FOR POLICY

Expanding Immigration Flows

Immigration has reemerged as a major challenge for U.S. social policy. During the past decade, changes in immigration law expanded the number of government-sanctioned immigrants allowed to enter and stay in the United States (Rolph, 1992). In addition, undocumented immigration appears to have continued unabated, despite laws against hiring undocumented workers (Woodrow and Passel, 1990; Crane et al., 1990). These flows will probably expand through the rest of this decade (Vernez, 1992). And despite the current recession, the United States continues to be an attractive destination; immigrants motivated by family unification or political and ethnic violence are seldom discouraged by U.S. economic conditions.

Recent immigration is already having substantial effects on the nation's demographic makeup (Vernez, 1992). Between 1980 and 1990, the number of foreign-born residents in the United States increased by 8.7 million. For some areas the impact has been proportionately greater. In Los Angeles, San Francisco, Dallas, Houston, few existing efforts that sample enough immigrants to be useful are either one-time surveys (which obviously cannot describe change over time) or conducted so infrequently that important changes are essentially ignored and causal relationships cannot be identified.

Fourth, most national data sets that have been major sources of information about immigrants (e.g., decennial census) have not used appropriate translations of the survey instrument for respondents with limited English skills. Many national surveys rely upon in-field translations of the English questionnaire and, hence, may yield data of uncertain quality on groups for whom English is not their first language. On-the-spot translations by interviewers or household members are inadequate for assuring comparability of data across language groups—or even within them. The absence of translated survey instruments may also result in samples that underrepresent those who do not speak English.

To see the combined effect of these shortcomings in design and procedure, consider the major data sources that immigration analyses are now forced to rely on:

The *decennial census*, which provides the data most commonly used to describe immigrants, identifies immigrants by country of birth,[1] but it provides no information about legal immigration status. The census also provides only a snapshot of the population every ten years, rather than the connected series of data over time that is needed to understand the dynamic process by which immigrants adapt. Although census data provide a limited capacity to compare foreign-born groups by the number of years they have lived in the United States, they do not allow researchers to examine the individual and family dynamics that are critical for answering such basic questions as how immigrants move into better jobs. Finally, the census does not cover immigrants who have returned to their home countries. Data about such individuals can indicate which support services are effective and which are not. They can also help develop a consensus about whether and when interventions are needed.

The *Current Population Survey* (CPS) has been used to estimate immigrants' labor force participation and family income. But because so few immigrants are included in each survey, analysts must combine information for several different years. This, combined with some of the flaws noted for census data, makes CPS data largely inadequate for understanding the adaptation process.

National sample survey efforts, such as the General Social Surveys, the National Longitudinal Surveys of Labor Market Participation, the National Longitudinal Survey of Youth, and High School and Beyond, often collect data on useful topics, but they rarely include enough immigrants for meaningful analysis. The Survey of Income and Program Participation, the Survey of Income and Education, and the Panel Study of Income Dynamics also suffer from inadequate numbers of immigrants in their samples.

---

[1]This approach misclassifies citizens born abroad.

Existing data sets cannot guide immigration policy. Although their collection efforts could conceivably be changed to provide more useful data on immigrants, an entirely new survey—designed specifically to give policymakers the information they need—would be more effective. Such an effort is clearly the best way to obtain data on large samples of immigrants at several points in time. It would also be a very effective way of addressing the problems of language and immigrant-specific data present in most current surveys.

Such a survey, especially on the national level, presents real methodological challenges. In the next two chapters we shall discuss these challenges.

Chapter Three

PILOT SURVEY DEVELOPMENT, PROCEDURES, AND STAFFING

OVERVIEW

Our pilot effort faced many of the same challenges that a national survey would confront, though on a smaller scale: deciding which immigrant populations to survey, recruiting and training bilingual staff, identifying neighborhoods where populations of interest are concentrated, developing and testing culturally appropriate survey instruments that can answer questions of concern, identifying individuals who qualify for the sample (which we accomplished using a short, separately administered screener), locating the same respondents again for a second interview, attempting to collect potentially sensitive information, and dealing with issues that arise in conducting the survey in several different immigrant communities at the same time.

We chose to survey Salvadorans and Filipinos for several reasons: (1) they represent the two continents from which most immigrants now come to the United States; (2) these populations are expected to grow, and they include recent arrivals as well as long-time residents; and (3) they have not been extensively studied. In developing the specific content of the survey, we focused on ascertaining and documenting the following:

- Immigration status (e.g., undocumented, temporary protected status, IRCA legalized, legal resident) and immigration history.

- Employment experiences, wages, and skills both before and after migration to the United States.

- Service needs and use for a broad range of public services, including health care, mental health, education, welfare, legal, and social services.

- Tax contributions.

- Family composition and economic transfers among non-coresident family members (including those in the home country).

- Use and ability level of English and of the home-country language (Spanish or Tagalog).

- Educational expectations and achievements of the immigrants themselves and their children.

The pilot survey had two phases: (1) a neighborhood screening to identify eligible respondents and (2) the main interview with these respondents. (The screener questionnaire, the main interview questionnaire, and the show cards for the latter are reproduced in Appendices A, B, and C, respectively.) Although, conceptually, the main questionnaire could have been administered immediately following the administration of the screener, the separation of these two efforts had several advantages for our pilot survey:

- Coming back several months later gave us the opportunity to address and gain insight into issues associated with fielding a *follow-up* survey.

- We could separate the training for the two parts of the survey, each of which, as noted below, entailed considerable effort. Our own and the interviewers' experiences during the screening phase gave us all a much better idea of what to expect during the main interview phase and to design training for that phase accordingly.

- We were able to adjust our sampling plans regarding which cases to pursue for the main interview to the number of potentially eligible cases that were screened.

Eligible households for the pilot study were identified using a short screening questionnaire in five Los Angeles County neighborhoods that had high concentrations of Salvadorans and Filipinos, according to data from the 1980 Census.[1] The sample was designed to yield at least 600 randomly selected Filipinos and Salvadorans (a total of 300 from each group). About 6,300 households were screened during a five-week period from May to June 1991 to identify eligible respondents (adults age 18 to 64 who were born in El Salvador or the Philippines); 1,161 eligible respondents were identified. If a household contained more than one eligible respondent, one was randomly selected (using the last-birthday method)[2] and asked to participate in a one-hour, in-home interview administered by a bilingual interviewer several months after the initial screening.

Like the screener, the questionnaire for the main interview was translated into Spanish and Tagalog.[3] It included a broad range of questions about the respondent and his/her family and their experiences living and working in the United States. The main questionnaire asked about the respondent's schooling and work history, migration history and status, family size and composition, the family's use of health care and public services, and the family's housing and expenses. Several items in the survey were highly sensitive, including questions about the respondent's legal (immigration) status, family income, and taxes. The designated respondent also

---

[1]The relevant information from the 1990 Census was not available when we selected our sample.

[2]Recently, many researchers have used birthday selection methods to randomly select respondents within sampling units (Lavarkas, 1987; Oldenick, Sorenson, Tuchfarber, and Bishop, 1985; O'Rourke and Blair, 1983; Salmon and Nichols, 1983). These methods either ask for the person within the sampling unit whose birthday was most recent or ask for the person who will have the next birthday. Because these birthday selection methods are nonintrusive, not time-consuming, and easy for interviewers to use, they are one of the most frequently used methods for random respondent selection.

[3]Tagalog is the principal dialect of Pilipino, the national language of the Philippines and the main language of Filipinos in Los Angeles.

served as a proxy for other family members since he/she was asked to provide fairly detailed information about the entire family.

Over a five-week survey period from August to September 1991, a team of 35 bilingual interviewers completed interviews with 655 respondents, including 382 Salvadorans and 273 Filipinos.

In this chapter we describe the procedures that we used during the pilot survey to (1) develop and translate the survey instruments, (2) sample eligible Filipino and Salvadoran immigrants in Los Angeles County, and (3) recruit, train, and supervise a bilingual interviewing staff.

DESIGNING, TRANSLATING, AND TESTING THE QUESTIONNAIRES

For each of the subject areas listed above, we reviewed existing questionnaires (e.g., for the decennial census, CPS, other surveys of immigrants) for ideas about specific question wording that might elicit the necessary information. We then translated both the screener and the main interview (as well as all field materials) into Spanish and Tagalog and pretested the translated instruments as well as the English versions.

This process required considerable work and attention to fine nuances in language to translate and pretest the questionnaires and culturally appropriate instruments (and associated field materials), in multiple languages (English, Spanish, and Tagalog) and on the same approximate schedule. Following usual research practice, we used the double translation technique (also called "back translation"). In this process, Translator A translates the original English version of the survey into the language of the target group. Then, Translator B translates the instrument back into English. The two English versions are compared to identify inconsistencies. If differences are found, the researcher overseeing the activity consults with both translators to reach a consensus about the best alternative, given the research objectives and characteristics of the study population (expected educational level, possible regional variations in language use).

To ensure that the pilot survey instruments were properly translated and that interviewers would be comfortable using them, we included a core group of the best interviewers for both language groups in the questionnaire translation and pretesting processes. We started with the traditional one-on-one pretest interviews with friends and acquaintances of the interviewers. In addition, we conducted several interviews with randomly selected respondents not known to the interviewers. After these procedures, we conducted group debriefing sessions with the interviewers and project staff and completed a question-by-question review of the translations. We worked in small groups to pinpoint areas where there was agreement about a translation problem, and then we retranslated questions as needed through a "group consensus development" approach. These efforts, while time-consuming, proved to be quite successful. After pretesting and refining the translations, we (and the interviewers) were reasonably confident about their quality.

We found that the Spanish translation and testing work were much more manageable than the Tagalog translation. There were two main reasons. First, one of our field supervisors and one of the principal investigators were bilingual in Spanish and English, and the former is a skilled translator. The bilingual field supervisor was also available to help with last-minute questionnaire changes and to translate the large volume of field materials into Spanish (letters, brochures, flyers, thank-you cards, change-of-address cards, question-and-answer sheets, show cards for the questionnaire, etc.), which minimized our reliance on an outside translator.

Second, the Spanish questionnaire was translated by someone who had successfully translated previous RAND surveys, so we had some shared understanding of what was expected with regard to degree of formality/informality and desired reading level for the target population.

With respect to the Tagalog translation, no one on the survey team other than the interviewers could read or speak Tagalog, which meant that we had to rely exclusively on outside translators and use interviewers to help validate the accuracy of the translation. We were unable to find a professional Tagalog translator with survey experience who also met our other work requirements.[4] After investigating several translation options, we opted for an agency to do the Tagalog translation.

As a test case, we asked the agency to translate the short screener interview into Tagalog before we made a final decision about using it for the longer, more complex, main questionnaire. This screening strategy paid off because the original screener translation was unusable: The interviewing staff described it as "literary" and "biblical" in style, not merely too formal. Fortunately, our staff included a Tagalog-speaking clerk, who was able to translate the screener to the satisfaction of the interviewers.

In retrospect, the overall questionnaire design process could have been improved if (1) more time had been allocated to pretesting and revising both the screener and main interview questionnaires in all three languages, including testing of individual items as well as the overall instrument in one-on-one interviews and in focus groups; and (2) translatability of questions was considered as measures were being developed, rather than after the design was completed in English. In most cases this can be accomplished if the research staff includes individuals familiar with the language and culture of the target populations from the beginning of the questionnaire design.

DRAWING A REPRESENTATIVE SAMPLE OF IMMIGRANTS

Issues in Drawing a Sample of Immigrants

Immigrants represent only a small share of the total population, and a sampling frame identifying them is not available.[5] Assembling a sample by randomly selecting households (especially nationwide), screening them to identify immigrants, and then

---

[4] The other requirements were access to a word processor that was compatible with RAND's system, to minimize the production typing work and costs, and ability to provide quick turnaround, e.g., 10 days for the questionnaire for the main interview.

[5] In the United States we do not have good information (e.g., population registers) to use as a sampling frame.

administering the main questionnaire only to immigrants would be extremely expensive. Targeting areas of immigrant concentration focuses resources and increases survey efficiency.

Any survey of immigrants requires a basic decision: should we sample from all foreign-born residents or only from certain immigrant communities? Focusing on a few carefully chosen groups permits larger subsamples from each country of origin— and allows for useful comparisons. But which groups to survey? Several factors must be considered. Survey designers might choose one group whose migration was motivated primarily by economic forces and another composed largely of political refugees, and compare the two. Language group may also influence the choice. For example, because we conducted the LACS in Spanish, we could have interviewed people from a number of different countries in Latin America. Our Tagalog questionnaire, in contrast, was usable only with Filipino immigrants. A new immigrant survey should probably include a Spanish-language sample and several Asian-language groups. One of the criteria we used to select study populations was the likelihood of additional large-scale immigration to the Los Angeles region. The Salvadoran and Filipino populations met this criterion.

Ideally one would like to have a representative sample of all members of the selected immigrant communities. Without a good sampling frame, however, our two alternatives were to do our own listing of addresses in the target area or to conduct a random-digit dialing of phone numbers in the target area. A telephone survey did not seem appropriate for interviewing immigrants both because of the likelihood that many immigrants might not have telephones (and hence could not be included in the sample) and because we felt person-to-person interviews and the use of show cards would greatly enhance the interviewers' ability to develop rapport with the respondents and to solicit answers to potentially sensitive questions. Given our conclusion that the best way to develop a sampling frame for drawing a representative sample of Filipinos and Salvadorans was to do our own listing of addresses, it would have been prohibitively expensive to try to draw a true random sample of all Filipinos and Salvadorans in Los Angeles.

How We Drew the LACS Sample of Immigrants

We originally planned to have a mix of purposively and randomly selected block groups within areas that have high densities of Filipinos and Salvadorans. However, for reasons described below, we ended up not interviewing households in the randomly selected areas. We did attempt to interview all households in the purposively selected areas, and hence our sample is representative of those areas.[6]

We used a three-stage sampling approach. First, we drew a purposive sample of census tracts based on their population densities in 1980[7] of Filipinos and non-Mexican

---

[6]The representativeness of our sample for Filipino and Salvadoran population in Los Angeles County is discussed in the next chapter.

[7]We relied on the 1980 Census tract data because the 1990 Census data were not available at the time and no other comparable sampling frame existed.

Hispanics (presumed to contain a significant proportion of Salvadorans). Second, we used a mixed purposive and random strategy within the high-density tracts, listing all living quarters in those areas. Third, we screened all listed residences in the target neighborhoods to identify eligible households. To be eligible a household had to contain at least one adult (age 18–64) who was born in El Salvador or the Philippines and who usually lived in the household. If there was more than one eligible adult in the household, one was randomly selected (using the last-birthday method) to be the primary respondent. For each community, we targeted 300 interviews.

Census tracts were initially identified from a sample of "high-density" non-Mexican Hispanic or Filipino zip codes in Los Angeles County. The zip codes were identified through community informants and other knowledgeables such as Salvadoran-oriented service agencies and Filipino newspapers. According to the 1980 Census, this "general target area," which is made up of 757 block groups,[8] contained 34 percent of all Filipinos and 33 percent of all non-Mexican Hispanics living in Los Angeles County. In 1980, the general target area contained an average of 25 Filipino households per thousand and about 80 non-Mexican Hispanic households per thousand. The Filipinos thus imposed the more severe constraint on the sample design. Within the general target area, there were two tracts in which the Filipino eligibility was estimated to be about 110 households per thousand.

We could not afford to list the entire target area to draw the sample, nor could we afford to send interviewers to random spots all over the target area. Because the distribution of both Filipinos and Salvadorans within this target area is very uneven, we would have faced a big risk of drawing a sample with an unacceptably low eligibility rate had we sampled tracts and blocks purely at random. Our initial plan was to use a "mixed" sample of 25 block groups, with some groups from the higher-density Salvadoran and Filipino block groups and others from randomly selected block groups in the general target area. This would permit us to achieve our targets for the number of interviews with the smallest field sample possible. To implement this plan, we selected a sample of block groups consisting of three strata:

- The three highest-density Filipino block groups,

- The two highest-density non-Mexican Hispanic block groups, and

- Twenty other block groups, selected at random from the remaining 752 block groups.

We expected these 25 block groups to contain 9,000 households, including 316 containing at least one adult born in the Philippines and 705 containing foreign-born "Other Hispanics."

We had several methodological and cost concerns about our sampling procedures, given the uncertainties surrounding the applicability of the 1980 Census data to 1991.

---

[8]A block group is a group of census blocks, usually about eight, although it is not uncommon to see as few as four and as many as sixteen. Groups of block groups make up census tracts; typically a census tract will contain from three to five block groups.

First, we had serious reservations about whether the eleven-year-old data would provide reasonable estimates of the number and location of Salvadorans and Filipinos. A second consideration was the high expected cost of the screening activities, given the large number of households to be screened to find enough eligible respondents. In addition to the overall costs of the screening operation, we were also concerned that costs for the Filipino sample in particular might be prohibitively high, since the expected eligibility rate for the overall target area was much lower than the Salvadoran sample, based on 1980 Census data (25 Filipino households per thousand, compared with 80 "non-Mexican Hispanic" households per thousand).

We were also concerned about possible difficulties in finding enough Salvadorans in the census tracts designated as "non-Mexican" or "Other" Hispanic. The census data did not provide precise counts for Salvadorans, but only aggregate counts of "Other Hispanics," who we presumed were primarily Salvadorans, because of our earlier neighborhood contacts and visits. As a backup, we also collected follow-up information for other Central Americans; in case we ran short of Salvadorans, we could still say something about Central American immigrants in this area. Finally, we realized that if the actual screener eligibility rates fell below our planning estimates, it would increase our screening costs considerably. For all these reasons, we decided to release the screening sample in small batches, starting with block groups within the five high-density tracts, in order to closely monitor planned versus actual eligibility rates, as well as screener costs.

However, when the field staff carried out a listing procedure that involved recording the addresses for all residences within the 25 selected block groups, it discovered many more residential addresses than expected—16,000 instead of 9,000 housing units—suggesting that there had been considerable new construction and population growth in these areas since the 1980 Census. To save costs, we decided to drop the 20 randomly selected low-density tracts from the sample, leaving an effective neighborhood screening sample of three high-density Salvadoran tracts and two high-density Filipino tracts with about 9,000 addresses. Observations during the listing confirmed that the high-density neighborhoods contained large proportions of Salvadorans and Filipinos. As the next chapter will describe, we eventually screened 6,300 of the 9,000 addresses in the five target neighborhoods.

RECRUITING, TRAINING, AND SUPERVISING A LARGE BILINGUAL INTERVIEWING STAFF

We were especially concerned about three key survey management issues. First, would it be difficult to recruit a large number of highly qualified bilingual interviewers (since normally it is extremely difficult to recruit nonwhite interviewers, especially males)? Second, would hiring and interviewer attrition be serious problems because the fieldwork was concentrated in many high-crime areas in Los Angeles County? Third, would our primarily English-speaking and female field supervisory staff encounter problems recruiting, training, and supervising a large bilingual field staff of both genders?

Below we discuss our overall approaches to interviewer recruitment, training, and supervision and the results of our pilot procedures.

Recruitment Procedures and Results

We were successful in recruiting a large, highly educated, and bilingual interviewing staff of both men and women. To allow for expected interviewer attrition, we initially sought to hire 20–25 bilingual interviewers for each sample group (Salvadoran and Filipino), with the expectation that about 75–80 percent of them would successfully complete training while the others would either self-select out or be terminated for performance problems. We wanted a primarily Latino and Filipino interviewing staff (with an even gender mix if possible), on the assumption that they would best be able to gain the trust of and establish rapport with immigrant families.

To identify applicants we posted job notices with a variety of organizations such as Filipino-American and Latino student groups at area colleges. We also contacted two temporary staff agencies that had recruited interviewers for RAND in the past. Students were surprisingly uninterested, perhaps because of the 20-hour-per-week minimum work requirement. By far the greatest response came from applicants who had seen advertisements placed by the temporary agencies in local newspapers. The agencies conducted the initial screening of applicants for basic skills, did routine checks on their past employers and their legal immigration status, and verified whether they had a valid driver's license, which was required for the job.

RAND staff then scheduled groups of ten to twelve applicants for group interviews, which gave us an opportunity to observe the personal interactions as well as to talk with the individual applicants. Applicants' language skills were evaluated by the Spanish-speaking RAND supervisor and a Filipina hired to work as both an interviewer and back translator. These evaluators, who were familiar with Central American and Filipino culture, were also able to evaluate whether candidates' interpersonal and communication skills were generally appropriate for our tasks.

The group interview sessions gave us a preview of the kinds of concerns survey respondents might have. The Latino applicants expressed concern about the purpose of the study, how we could guarantee confidentiality, and how the survey data would be used. The Filipino applicants were less concerned about these issues, and they tended to react positively that a study was focusing on their community. Many applicants predicted that respondents might be suspicious and unwilling to divulge sensitive information, especially immigration status. It was clear that training would need to include a question-and-answer session with the assistance of the research staff to assure the interviewers of our intentions, so that they in turn could persuade respondents to participate.

Altogether, 80 applicants (40 Spanish speaking and 40 Tagalog speaking) were screened in English, of whom 35 (44 percent) were eventually hired and served as interviewers: 21 of the Spanish speakers and 14 of the Tagalog speakers. Of the 35 interviewers, 60 percent had completed four years of college, one-third had some college experience, and the rest had completed high school. Table 3.1 presents data on the gender, employment status, nationality, and education of the interviewers.

Although we were comfortable with the overall quality of the applicants selected and their fluency in Spanish or Tagalog, we had some other concerns. First, the English-speaking skill level of more than half those hired was below that which we would generally require for general population surveys. We were concerned that this situation might create communication problems for the training and supervisory staff, most of whom were not bilingual.

Second, of the 35 interviewers hired, only eight (22 percent) were women. Very few women applied for the interviewing job; many who inquired about the position indicated they felt the areas where they would be working were unsafe. The fact that we did not offer to provide escorts or suggest that interviewers could work in pairs may also have discouraged many women from applying for the job. We were very concerned about the implications of a predominately male interviewing staff, knowing that many female respondents might hesitate to open their doors to unknown men, and knowing that most survey organizations usually find it quite difficult to recruit and retain male interviewers, especially members of minority groups.

Third, only a few of those hired had survey interviewing experience (about 20 percent). Many had some door-to-door experience working with the public and some had done academic research of some sort in their home countries, but few had the level of relevant interviewing experience we would normally want. Of the 35, only

Table 3.1

Characteristics of the Interviewers Hired for the Los Angeles Community Survey

	Salvadoran	Filipino	Total
Total interviewers	21	14	35
Gender			
Male	17	10	27
Female	4	4	0
Employment status			
Full-time or part-time at other job	12	12	24
In school	3	0	3
Not working or in school	6	2	8
Nationality			
Born in U.S.	8	3	11
Born in Philippines	0	11	11
Born in El Salvador	3	0	3
Born in Mexico, other Central American or other Spanish-speaking country	10	0	10
Education level			
High school only	1	1	2
Some college	10	2	12
College degree	10	11	21

one (a Salvadoran woman) had extensive personal interviewing experience (with the U.S. Census Bureau). This meant that we had a large group of bilingual interviewers with little or no professional interviewing experience, for whom English was their second language, and who were somewhat apprehensive at the start about their ability to convince Salvadoran and Filipino residents to divulge sensitive information about themselves in a survey.

Overall, these concerns proved to be less problematic than we feared, but they did have a noticeable impact on the content and structure of our interviewer-training programs and the level of field supervision required. For the most part, the interviewers' overall performance far exceeded our expectations, and their outstanding efforts in the field were largely responsible for the success of the pilot.

Interviewer attrition was not a serious problem, but the dropout rate was higher with the Salvadoran-sample interviewers, who were working in much more difficult neighborhoods. Of the 21 Salvadoran-sample interviewers who were hired, seven quit voluntarily and one was let go, for an overall attrition rate of 33 percent over a period of two to three months. Most of this attrition occurred early: two quit at the end of screener training, three left after one week in the field, and the remaining two left later in the survey period. Only two of the fourteen Filipino interviewers quit during the field period, for an attrition rate of 14 percent during the same two to three months. In most cases, the interviewers who quit cited time conflicts with their other commitments (work or school) as the reason.

Interviewer Training

We faced several challenges in designing an effective interviewer-training program for the bilingual interviewers. We had a large group of bilingual interviewers and a small, primarily English-speaking training staff. The lead trainers were not bilingual, and most of the training was designated to be conducted in English. At least half of the interviewers were more comfortable reading and speaking in their native language. We had a large and complex screening operation and a long, complicated main interview, so considerable training on general interviewing techniques, as well as on project-specific requirements, was needed to perform the fieldwork accurately. We also had to allot time for interviewers to break into language-specific groups to review and practice the translated instruments. We allocated some training time to discuss different approaches for contacting respondents and gaining their cooperation. Additionally, most of the interviewers had other job commitments, limiting their availability to evenings and weekends. Because many interviewers were working full-time jobs, we found that their capacity to absorb several hours of new material night after night was somewhat lower than we had hoped.

Initially we planned to conduct a five-day training program (approximately 32 hours of training) covering both the screener and main interview. However, we opted to separate the interviewer training (and fieldwork) into two phases—screener training and main interview training—making it much more manageable. First, we trained on the screener and allowed interviewers to complete the entire screening operation in about five weeks. Then, after interviewers had successfully completed the screener and after a break of 2–3 weeks, while the questionnaire for the main interview was finalized,[9] we trained the interviewers on the longer, more complex main questionnaire. Altogether, we found it took us 48 hours to train interviewers on both the screener and main interview.

Training for the Screener. The 24 hours of screener training included four four-hour classroom sessions, three one-hour paid homework assignments, a couple of open-book quizzes, and a debriefing/retraining session after one week in the field. Most training was conducted with the entire group of 35, but we did break into smaller language-specific groups for extensive role-playing and practice sessions and to review the translated questionnaire and associated materials.

The first session began with an in-depth discussion with the principal investigators about the purpose and background of the study. This reassured the previously somewhat skeptical interviewing staff, who had concerns about how a RAND study could affect their communities. It set a very positive tone for the rest of training and no doubt contributed to the remarkably high level of commitment we saw in most of the interviewers throughout the field period. It was also essential to the success of the fieldwork, in that interviewers could confidently and sincerely persuade respondents to participate.

The screener training also included a session on general interviewing skills. Even though some of these skills would not be used until the main interview several months later, it gave us an opportunity to understand better the interviewers' abilities and to reinforce the relevant skills during the main interview training. We also had a lengthy session on refusals and other potential respondent problems, led by a field director with considerable experience working with diverse cultural groups.

The screening protocols and procedures were presented verbally, with extensive use of easy-to-read overhead slides and at a relatively slow pace, to make it easier to follow. The materials were also provided in written form in the interviewer's manuals so the interviewers could review them on their own as well.

When we discussed the translated materials during training, we were fortunate with the Spanish-speaking group because our bilingual supervisor could facilitate group discussions of the translations. The Tagalog-speaking interviewers were at a clear disadvantage because we did not have a Tagalog-speaking supervisor or consultant qualified to lead these discussions. We relied, instead, on the English-speaking supervisor and field director, who attempted to carry out review sessions with the Filipino interviewers. While we encouraged discussion in Tagalog, most Filipinos, out of politeness and respect for the supervisor, spoke mostly English during the training.

Training for the Main Interview. Training for the main interview consisted of five four-hour classroom sessions plus several hours of paid home study, for a total training time of around 24 hours per interviewer. Copies of the English version of the

---

[9]Some of the interviewers helped field test the questionnaire for the main interview during this "break." Most of the other interviewers welcomed this break as a chance to catch up on other things (such as their full-time jobs).

questionnaire were mailed in advance to the interviewers, with instructions to read it, review the general interviewing skills manual, and then conduct an interview with someone they knew, so that they arrived at training familiar with the survey content.

Overall, the interviewers surprised us by learning our complicated questionnaire very quickly. They seemed to approach the main interviewing job far more confidently because they had been largely successful in their screener activities. (The response rates for the screener are discussed in the next chapter.) We used the same basic approach to training that was used during the screener: a slow-paced briefing style with overhead slides that emphasized key concepts, special definitions, major skip patterns, expected respondent questions, etc., and lots of time for role-playing and practice exercises. We also administered two quizzes during training to help us gauge how well interviewers understood critical concepts.

Field Supervisory Procedures and Experiences

Supervisory Procedures. The 21 interviewers for the Salvadoran sample were supervised by a field supervisor who was familiar with Central American culture, had prior experience supervising interviewers, was bilingual, and was herself Mexican. The 14 Filipino sample interviewers were supervised by a field supervisor who had personal interviewing experience but did not know Tagalog and had no special knowledge of Filipino culture. To fill this language gap, we hired a Filipino survey clerk to assist with minor translations, answer respondent telephone inquiries, help us to develop a good rapport with the interviewers, and serve as an informal resource person on cultural issues.

The supervisors spent considerable time in the field observing the screening operation and giving the interviewers feedback on how to complete the work in an organized and efficient manner. The supervisors met the interviewers in the field during the first week of screening. They observed each interviewer as he/she completed several screening interviews and associated paperwork. Not surprisingly, the interviewers in both language groups needed considerable assistance during the early stages of the screener because most had no previous experience doing professional interviewing and handling many paperwork tasks.

During the screener and main interview phases, interviewers received assignments that we estimated would take them one to two weeks to complete. Interviewers were free to work on their own schedules within certain guidelines: They could not begin before 3:30 p.m. or later than 9:00 p.m. during the week, and they had to work either on Saturday or Sunday each week. We asked interviewers to work a minimum of 20 hours per week, but the actual time worked turned out to range from 12 to 36 hours per week. They called in weekly to report their progress in terms of numbers of completed cases, refusals, cases in progress, etc. Every ten days to two weeks they either came into the office or were met in the field by their supervisors to turn in completed work and to receive additional assignments.[10]

---

[10]Ideally, interviewers would have reported to their supervisors in the office in person on a weekly basis. However, most of the interviewers lived long distances from RAND, as well as from their field assignments,

There were real drawbacks to having the interviewers visit the central office biweekly rather than weekly. Receiving completed cases every ten days to two weeks caused delays in notifying interviewers of their errors and in validating their work as quickly as possible. More frequent personal contact with interviewers would have helped improve the overall effort, but would also have reduced the time they had available to conduct interviews. In retrospect, some combination of frequent mail-ins, in-person visits, and supervisor site visits would have been optimal to ensure that survey editing and validation were conducted on an ongoing basis with continual feedback to interviewers.

Validation Procedures and Results. Following standard survey practice, a random sample of each interviewer's work was validated by RAND supervisors during both the screener and main interview phases. Our overall strategy for maintaining quality control over interviewers' work included four core components: (1) intense on-site observation of interviewers' work, especially during the larger screening operation; (2) reinterviewing a sample of respondents by telephone (or in person) to validate interviewers' work by reasking key questions from the survey; (3) validating a sample of screener cases coded as "ineligible" to confirm the accuracy of the information supplied by interviewers; and (4) randomly reassigning at least 20–25 percent of each interviewer's completed eligible screeners to another interviewer as a further validation measure to ensure that the data were valid.

Only one minor validation problem turned up during the screener phase, which was not completely unexpected. We found that one Salvadoran-sample interviewer had falsified about twenty screeners with various ineligible disposition codes (cases coded as business, vacancies, etc.).

During the main interview phase, 20 percent of each interviewer's completed interviews were validated by telephone. No validation problems turned up on the Salvadoran sample, but there were serious problems involving three of the Filipino interviewers. During the main interview's third week of fielding, we discovered that three Filipino interviewers had falsified cases. We attempted to validate 100 percent of their work by telephone or in person, and successfully reached 75 percent of the respondents. One interviewer clearly falsified all his data, while the other two falsified approximately one-fourth of their cases.[11] These three interviewers denied having falsified cases but were clearly upset by our discovery.[12]

While it is true that most Filipino interviewers were successful in gaining respondent cooperation on balance, the Filipino interviewers, by conventional survey standards, did not perform up to the level anticipated and did not demonstrate (to the full satis-

---

so a trip to RAND for a meeting usually required at least 1–2 hours commuting time each way for the typical interviewer, who was also working another full-time or part-time job.

[11]Additionally, the same three Filipino interviewers who falsified data, plus a fourth Filipino interviewer, kept about 50 grocery certificates that were intended as respondent payments (discussed in Chapter Four), even when the interviews took place. Two of the four admitted to keeping the certificates and repaid us for them, but the other two denied taking them.

[12]Fowler (1988) points out that validation problems such as those encountered during our pilot seem to occur most often with newly hired interviewers. However, organizations with experienced professional staff also routinely check a sample of their work to guard against possible "faked data."

faction of their supervisor) that their work was up to par with the Salvadoran-sample interviewers. The English-speaking supervisor who observed their work in the field generally gave them much lower performance ratings for basic interviewing skills, interpersonal skills, probing, proper recording of answers, completing assignments on time, and following administrative procedures. Compared with the Salvadoran interviewers, fewer Filipinos received an "excellent" or "good" performance rating, and five of the fourteen received a "below average" rating (see Table 3.2).

It is important to note, however, that our assessments of the Filipino interviewers were based on how well they performed in English. If we had had the added knowledge of how well they performed in Tagalog, it might have influenced (positively or negatively) our overall assessments. But since most of the actual Filipino interviews were conducted in English (about 60 percent), we felt that our performance assessments were a reasonably accurate measure of how well the Filipinos did as interviewers.

Table 3.2

Supervisor Ratings of Interviewer Performance

Rating	Salvadoran	Filipino
Excellent	10%	7%
Good	47%	29%
Average	33%	29%
Below average	10%	35%

Chapter Four

LESSONS LEARNED FROM THE PILOT SURVEY

By and large, the experiences and field results of the LACS provide support for the feasibility of a national immigrant survey. This section describes how the household-screening procedures and participation in the main interview went and how complete and reliable the answers appeared to be.

HOW WELL DID THE HOUSEHOLD SCREENING PROCEDURES WORK?

To assess the success of the screener procedures, we examined field results through several measures. First, we monitored the household enumeration (listing) process closely to determine whether any unique problems emerged at this stage of the fieldwork. Second, we examined the screener response rates and compared the experiences of the Salvadoran and Filipino samples. Besides screener participation rates, we also reviewed other indicators of the respondents' willingness to participate, including whether or not they provided family members' names, phone numbers, and other information to permit us to randomly select and interview one eligible adult in each eligible household.

Overall the screener worked quite well, but there were several unexpected results, as described below.

The Field Listing Process

As noted in the previous chapter, we grossly underestimated the number of residential addresses in the target census block groups and, therefore, underestimated the potential cost of the screening operation, given the low eligibility rates, about 19 percent (see below). There was a dramatic increase in the overall number of residences since the 1980 Census, as well as in the number of eligible foreign-born Filipinos and Salvadorans in the selected areas. Nonetheless, the listing of 16,000 addresses in the target census block groups in Los Angeles County was a fairly inexpensive component of the pilot field operations. It took about 30 person-days (not counting supervisory time) to complete this work.

We subsequently discovered, however, that the field lister had made many errors in the address listing, many of which had to be corrected by the interviewers during the screening phase. The listing problems were concentrated primarily in the densely populated Salvadoran census tracts, which had a large number of apartment buildings with many hidden housing units (e.g., units above garages/businesses that were not always visible from the street).

We attribute this listing problem to the fact that the field lister, who was not bilingual, did not adequately investigate apartment buildings in high-crime areas. He therefore missed a number of housing units, which sometimes contained eligible immigrants. Additionally, some listings were more than six months old by the time the screening process began, and in several cases entire buildings had been torn down and even replaced with new ones.

Screener Response Rates

Table 4.1 describes the response rates and reasons for nonresponse in each community. The sample for screening purposes consisted of 6,333 listed addresses, clustered in two high-density Salvadoran census block groups with 4,155 units and three high-density Filipino block groups with 2,178 units. Subsequently, 374 addresses were found to be ineligible because the units were vacant or nonresidences (e.g., businesses). An additional 245 addresses were also deleted from the sample because interviewers found that no such address existed (e.g., the apartment building

Table 4.1

Final Disposition of the Screener Sample

	Salvadoran Block Groups	Filipino Block Groups	Total Cases
Listed/issued cases	4,155	2,178	6,333
Nonresidences			
Vacancy	254	75	329
Not a residence	30	15	45
No such address	213	32	245
Total	497	122	619
Residences			
Completes	1,928	1,415	3,343
Breakoffs	35	38	73
Refusals	281	161	442
Language barrier	131	11	142
Illness/senility	19	4	23
Inaccessible	588	82	670
Maximum calls	178	75	253
Field period ended	431	204	635
Other	67	66	133
Total	3,658	2,056	5,714
Response rates	52.7% (1,928/3,658)	68.8% (1,415/2,056)	58.5% (3,343/5,714)
Refusal/breakoff rates	8.62% (316/3,658)	9.7% (199/2,056)	9.0% (515/5,714)

had been demolished). Of the remaining 5,714 presumably residential households, screeners were completed for 3,343, for an overall response rate of 59 percent.[1] About one-third of the successfully screened households contained an eligible respondent. There was a total of 1,161 eligible households, including 637 Salvadorans and 524 Filipinos.

Response rates to the screener differ considerably for the two communities, averaging 53 percent for the Salvadoran block groups and 69 percent for the Filipino block groups. The major factor contributing to the lower Salvadoran response rate was the large percentage of units in inaccessible apartment buildings. About 16 percent of the Salvadoran sample, compared with only 4 percent of the Filipino sample, could not be screened because interviewers could not gain access to locked or security buildings.[2] Refusal rates were relatively low—around 9 percent—for each community.

Overall, a small percentage of the sample could not be successfully screened due to language barriers (e.g., non-English-speaking Asian immigrants such as Koreans or Vietnamese). Most of the language problems were concentrated in the Salvadoran tracts, which were more likely to include immigrant groups that did not speak English or Spanish. Nearly 4 percent of the residences in the Salvadoran neighborhoods received a final status code of "language barrier," whereas less than 1 percent of the residences in the Filipino neighborhoods fell into this category.

We terminated the screening operations after roughly five weeks, when the pool of eligible cases was close to 1,200, or approximately twice as many households as desired for the main interview. We used the 2:1 ratio as a conservative hedge against the likelihood that these households would not participate in the main interview.

About 16 percent of the sample (close to 900 cases) received a final status of "maximum calls" or "field period ended" because we did not have the time or resources to allow interviewers to track down the more-difficult-to-locate respondents. Interviewers were generally instructed to make no more than four attempts (scheduled on different days of the week and at different times of the day) to interview respondents. Interviewers could, of course, make more callbacks than this if they happened to be in the area for their other assignments. For the most part, the Filipino screener sample, which was much smaller than the Salvadoran screener sample, received more contacts, which accounts in part for the higher response rates for the Filipino sample. The interviewer time per completed screener household

---

[1]By completed screener, we mean that an adult in the household finished the screener and provided the interviewer with the information needed to determine household eligibility. The screener could be completed by any adult household member. No incentive payments were offered for participating in the screener. However, eligible households were told that they would receive a $5.00 grocery certificate for participating in the one-hour main interview.

[2]Interviewers were generally successful at gaining access to security apartment buildings. However, there were a few very large apartment buildings in the Salvadoran tracts where the manager refused to allow the interviewers in. Refusals from three apartment managers accounted for close to 600 addresses that could not be successfully screened in the Salvadoran neighborhoods.

averaged about 40 minutes per case[3] for both the Filipino and Salvadoran samples, which was close to the original planning estimates.

The response rates to the LACS screener are roughly comparable to those commonly obtained on personal interviewing surveys in inner cities, and in Los Angeles in particular,[4] and are consistent with the fact that response rates are generally good among Hispanic populations.[5] Our low refusal rates and credible response rates to the LACS screener were particularly impressive considering that we did not make special efforts to attempt to convert first refusals to responses or to do extensive follow-up of difficult-to-reach respondents.[6] Furthermore, we did not even attempt to contact over 10 percent of the listed cases because the field period ended.[7]

We attribute the overall high level of respondent cooperation during the screener to several key factors. First, the screener was very brief and easy to administer: on average it took about five minutes to administer, and any adult household member could complete it. Since the interview was short, most respondents were willing to complete the screener right away rather than schedule appointments for a later time.

Second, the bilingual interviewers were effective in persuading reluctant respondents to complete the short screener—even if it had to be done on the front steps rather than in the home. Conducting the screener in the language preferred by the respondent was also an important factor in soliciting a favorable response from immigrant households.

Third, our interviewers were comfortable working in the immigrant neighborhoods, even those that were clearly high-crime areas, and they were persistent in their efforts to locate and interview sample members. There was only one reported case where a Salvadoran interviewer did not attempt to contact residents in a sampled unit out of concern for his safety. (He was warned by neighbors that a gang had moved into the vacant unit and should be avoided.) This experience was particularly impressive because survey organizations have found it increasingly difficult to find

---

[3]This figure includes actual interviewing time, plus travel time, callbacks, and time spent on administrative tasks (e.g., filling out productivity reports, weekly meetings, etc.). It does not include interviewer time for training or time for field supervision.

[4]Response rates to personal interview surveys in Los Angeles tend to run somewhere between 60 and 70 percent, depending on the intensity of follow-up with difficult-to-reach respondents (personal communication with Eve Fielder, director of the UCLA Institute for Survey Research, which conducts many household surveys in the Los Angeles area). Fowler (1988) indicates that "academic survey organizations are usually able to achieve response rates in the 75 percentage range" for general population surveys. He points out, however, that response rates are usually lower in central cities than they are in rural or suburban areas, primarily because of difficulties locating respondents and access problems in inner cities.

[5]Marín and VanOss Marín (1991) indicate that response rates among Mexican-Americans and other Hispanic groups nationwide tend to be somewhat higher than those obtained on general population surveys. Refusal rates among Hispanics are typically quite low (consistently under 10 percent), according to Marín and VanOss Marín's review of past research with Hispanic populations. Indeed, UCLA's experience has been that Mexican-Americans tend to be at the higher end of the response rate continuum compared with non-Hispanic white populations. It appears that non-Mexican "Other Hispanic" populations also cooperate at levels comparable to the Mexican-American population in the Southwest.

[6]Nationally, response rates have been declining, particularly in urban areas. This appears primarily to be a function of increasing refusal rates (Steeh, 1981).

[7]If we exclude such cases from the denominator, the response rates would be 60 percent and 76 percent for the Salvadoran and Filipino block groups, respectively, and 66 percent overall.

interviewers who are comfortable working in high-crime central cities where visits at night are required.[8]

Fourth, the clustering of the sample and the interviewers in a few target neighborhoods facilitated our efforts to persuade families to participate in the survey. Because groups of interviewers were screening many units in designated census blocks and leaving brightly colored information flyers (see Appendix D) about the survey throughout neighborhoods and apartment buildings, local residents who were initially reluctant to participate (e.g., they may have refused to open their door when the first contact was made) soon learned that they had not been singled out and that many of their neighbors had already spoken to the interviewers. The information flyers, which were left in respondents' mailboxes or on their doorsteps when they were not home, proved to be an effective way of introducing the study to local residents.

Other Indicators of Respondent Cooperation During Screening

In addition to determining household eligibility, interviewers also attempted during the screener to complete the random selection of respondents (within eligible families) at the same time. Interviewers were extremely successful in completing short household rosters at the time of the screener (that is, asking for family members' first names or initials, gender, age, and country of origin) and were able to complete the respondent selection process in practically all cases.

Further evidence of the cooperation received from most Filipino and Salvadoran residents during the screening interview is the large percentage of respondents in both groups who provided the name and phone number for the randomly selected respondent. Of the eligible households, 99 percent provided full (or partial) names and 84 percent gave phone numbers so that interviewers could contact the selected respondent at a later date.

PARTICIPATION IN THE MAIN INTERVIEW

We entered the main interview phase of the pilot with six basic methodological concerns:

- Would respondents who were cooperative during the screener participate in a one-hour in-home interview that included some questions on sensitive topics?

- Could we interview the *selected* respondent?

---

[8]For example, at the May 1992 Field Directors' Conference in St. Petersburg, Florida, a panel of survey researchers from the major academic and government survey organizations in the United States discussed the special problems of inner-city interviewing. Much of that discussion focused on two key issues: (1) the extensive community outreach and publicity efforts that are commonly needed to solicit a high level of community and individual cooperation (and to facilitate recruitment of minority staff); and (2) the strategies used to recruit and retain minority staff to help minimize recruitment problems and high staff turnover (such as offering higher salaries and benefits, bonuses, special training on safety issues, paid escorts or helpers in high-crime areas, use of community informants and resource persons to survey neighborhoods and assess their safety levels prior to interviewing, and so forth).

- Would nonresponse be selective? That is, how representative would our sample be of the targeted populations?

- How much effort would it take to locate and interview the selected respondents?

- How important would incentive payments be in encouraging survey participation? In particular, would a $5.00 grocery certificate be an effective incentive payment?

- Would a large fraction of selected respondents move before we recontacted them, since there was an average lag of nine weeks between the screener and main interview?

Below we discuss what we learned about each of these survey issues during the pilot.

Response Rates for the Main Interview

Over a five-week period, a field staff of 35 interviewers attempted to interview the 637 Salvadoran and 524 Filipino respondents identified as eligible during the screening phase. As shown in Table 4.2, we exceeded our completion target of 300 for the Salvadoran sample but fell slightly short of our goal for the Filipino sample, for reasons we shall outline below.

Of the 637 eligible Salvadoran cases in the main interview sample, we obtained completed interviews from 382 respondents, for an overall response rate of 60 percent. Refusal rates were remarkably low, averaging only 5 percent for the Salvadoran sample. Most of the nonresponse for the Salvadoran sample was due to three factors: the fairly large number of respondents/families who moved (11 percent), the

Table 4.2

Disposition of the Main Interview Sample

	Salvadoran Cases		Filipino Cases		Total Cases	
	N	Percent	N	Percent	N	Percent
Cases identified as eligible from the screening interview	637	100.0	524	100.0	1,161	100.0
Completes	382	60.0	273	52.1	655	56.4
Refusal/breakoff	32	5.0	42	8.0	74	6.4
Moved[a]	71	11.1	12	2.3	83	7.1
Vacancy	4	0.6	0	0.0	4	0.3
Inaccessible/illness/language barrier/ unavailable for other reasons	8	1.3	13	2.5	21	1.8
Maximum calls	67	10.5	13	2.5	80	6.9
Field period ended	66	10.4	73	13.9	139	12.0
Interviewer error/validation problems[b]	7	1.1	98	18.7	105	9.0

[a]The "moved" category includes selected respondents who moved as well as entire households that moved.

[b]The "interviewer error/validation problems" category includes cases where (1) the wrong respondent was interviewed, (2) interviewers falsified data, and (3) other interviewer errors occurred, such as the wrong person being selected as the respondent in the screener.

fact that some respondents were not contacted at all before the field period ended (10 percent), and the limited number of callbacks (usually no more than four) that interviewers made to 11 percent of the sample who potentially could have been interviewed had the field period been extended and the number of callbacks increased. We ended the field period in five weeks, and 133 Salvadoran-sample cases received a final status code of "maximum calls" or "field period ended," bypassing an extensive follow-up. Furthermore, we did not attempt to track respondents (71 cases) who had moved. With more time and resources for the field data collection, we think that the overall response rates for both the Salvadoran and Filipino samples could have been increased by at least 10 percentage points.

In the Filipino sample, we completed interviews with 273 out of 524 eligible cases, for an overall response rate of 56 percent. As with the screener, refusal rates were quite low, averaging about 8 percent. Unlike the Salvadoran sample, high mobility rates were not a problem, since only 2 percent of the Filipino respondents/families had moved since the screener was completed.

Two major factors account for the low response rates in the Filipino sample. One was the short field period (14 percent of the eligible respondents were never contacted), and the other was the serious interviewer "curbstoning" (cheating) problem that was identified late in the field period and discussed in Chapter Three: during routine validation checks, field supervisors discovered that three of the sixteen Filipino interviewers had falsified part of the data for a sample of their completed cases. Unfortunately, these three interviewers were among the highest producers on the interviewing team, accounting for nearly one-third of the Filipino sample. The usual survey practice under such circumstances is to reassign problem validation cases to another interviewer to complete, but we did not do this during the pilot because of budget and schedule constraints.[9]

Did We Interview the Randomly Selected Respondent?

As seen in Table 4.3, the majority of the households that completed the main interview contained more than one eligible respondent. Nonetheless, with few exceptions, interviewers succeeded in interviewing the adult who had been randomly selected during the screening interview.

Interviewers had been apprehensive about their ability to convince respondents of the need to interview the selected respondent, rather than any adult in the household. These concerns stemmed in large part from interviewers' fears that in male-headed Salvadoran and Filipino households they would encounter problems from husbands if the wives were selected for the interview. During the first week of interviewing, there were several instances where interviewers encountered some resis-

---

[9]When we exclude from the denominator the cases that were not contacted ("field period ended") and those with validation problems, response rates are 67.7 percent for the Salvadoran sample, 77.3 percent for the Filipinos, and 71.4 percent overall.

Table 4.3

**Number of Eligible Respondents per Household Identified
in Screener Interview**

Number of Eligible Respondents in Household	Salvadorans	Filipinos
1	25%	11%
2	39	35
3	20	24
4	10	14
5	4	10
6	1	3
7	1	1
8	0	1
9	0	1
Total	100	100
N	382	273

tance from respondents, but most interviewers were quite successful in interviewing the designated respondent. We encountered only nine cases in which the interviewer clearly interviewed someone other than the designated respondent.[10]

How Representative Is Our Sample of the Targeted Populations?

We used data from the 1990 Census to assess how our sample compares to the Salvadoran and Filipino immigrant populations enumerated for Los Angeles County. The key characteristics compared include gender, age, marital status, education, and length of time in the United States.

Table 4.4 indicates that our respondents are generally similar with regard to gender, distribution by age, and length of time in the United States to the general Salvadoran and Filipino immigrant population residing in Los Angeles County in 1990. Our sampled respondents were somewhat more likely to be married than the overall immigrant population of Los Angeles County.[11] Another exception is that our Filipino respondents were somewhat more likely not to have completed high school than the Los Angeles County Filipino immigrant population in general. However, the education level of our Salvadoran respondents is similar to that of the overall Salvadoran immigrant community in Los Angeles County.

By and large, we conclude that a representative sample of the general immigrant population of a large area can be drawn by concentrating on high-density immigrant areas. However, to assure representativeness, a full survey ought also to randomly sample areas of lower immigrant density, as we had originally planned.

---

[10]These cases are not included in the count of completed cases.

[11]As noted earlier, this "bias" may have resulted from our female respondents' reluctance to be interviewed without another family member present. In future surveys, adequate representation of female interviewers is needed to minimize this potential bias.

Table 4.4

Comparison of Socio-Demographic Characteristics of Survey Samples and Salvadoran and Filipino Immigrant Communities of Los Angeles County

Characteristics	Salvadoran Immigrants		Filipino Immigrants	
	Survey Sample	L.A. County	Survey Sample	L.A. County
Gender				
Females	55%	51%	54%	56%
Age				
18–29	47	42	19	23
30–44	42	42	39	38
Marital status				
Married	62	48	75	62
Education				
No high school	79	71	30	12
High school graduate	17	15	2	13
Bachelor's degree or more	1	2	50	47
Time in United States				
Entered within last 10 years	74	81	44	49

SOURCES: RAND and 1990 Census.

How Much Effort Did It Take to Locate and Interview Selected Respondents?

To assess the level of effort required to survey immigrants, we analyzed indicators of the four main components of the field procedures: interviewer productivity rates (time per completed interview), length of the interview, number of visits required to complete the interview, and contact procedures (use of advance phone calls to arrange appointments versus unannounced home visits). Our results are tabulated in Table 4.5.

Table 4.5

Effort Required to Complete Interviews

Average total interviewer time per case	3.8 hours
Interview time range	25–125 minutes
Interview time	
<45 minutes	20%
45–60 minutes	60%
>60 minutes	20%
Interview attempts	
1	50%
2	23%
3	14%
4	7%
5 or more	6%

while until they had established a positive rapport with the respondent before mentioning the gift certificate. They felt it was far more effective to first explain why the survey was important to the Salvadoran community and then offer the payment at a later point in the interview as a "thank you" gesture for the respondent's participation.

The Filipino-sample interviewers, who were initially quite concerned about offering respondent payments, used a totally different tactic for presenting gift certificates. Usually they did not mention the certificate at all until after the interview was over, and then they stressed that it was merely a small token of appreciation. With few exceptions, most Filipino respondents did not appear to be offended and readily accepted the gift certificates as a polite "thank you" gift rather than as a payment for services.

Although most interviewers and respondents accepted the concept of a respondent payment, we found that a few of the Filipino respondents and interviewers had problems with this procedure. A small number of Filipino respondents declined the payments, reportedly because they either were offended or felt they did not need the gift certificate. As discussed in Chapter Three, we also discovered during our random validation checks that four interviewers did not offer the certificates to their respondents. Two of the four admitted to keeping the certificates and repaid us for them, but the other two denied taking them.

Respondent Mobility Between the Screening and Main Interview: Implications for Tracking Respondents in a Longitudinal Survey

The median length of time between the screening interview and the main interview was nine weeks.[13] As noted above, only 2 percent of respondents in the Filipino sample moved during the period between the interviews, but the mobility rate was 11 percent among the Salvadorans—a high rate for such a short period of time. The mobility rate for the Salvadoran sample is roughly comparable to the experiences of Marín and VanOss Marín (1991) in San Francisco, who found that it was possible to recontact 87 percent of Hispanics interviewed 30 days after the initial interview. However, that study reports that some researchers have experienced attrition rates as high as 45 percent among highly mobile urban Hispanics who are recontacted one year after the initial survey.[14]

As noted above, 84 percent of respondents to the screener gave phone numbers so that interviewers could contact the selected respondent at a later date. To test respondents' general willingness to provide tracking information for possible longitudinal followups, we also asked the screener respondent to give us the name, address, and/or phone number of at least one friend or relative just in case they moved before we returned (in a month or two) to complete the main interview.

---

[13]For 10 percent of the completed cases, less than 7 weeks elapsed between the screener and the main interview, while for another 10 percent this figure exceeded 11.5 weeks.

[14]For an in-depth discussion of approaches for maintaining contact with Hispanic survey participants in a longitudinal study, see Marín and VanOss Marín (1991).

Twenty-eight percent of the screener respondents provided this additional tracking information at the time of the brief screener interview (although we do not know the completeness and reliability of this tracking information since we did not attempt to track pilot families who moved). These questions were asked early in the screener interview, before the interviewer had an opportunity to establish much of a rapport with the respondent. We think that the response rates for these questions would have been considerably greater had they been included at the end of the main interview, when greater rapport and trust had been established with the respondent.

As a further tracking strategy, we also left a change-of-address card with each screener respondent and asked him/her to return it to RAND if he/she moved. This strategy was not effective. Although about 80 respondents moved between the time of the screener and the main interview (a lag of about 7–11 weeks for most respondents), only four of them returned an address update card.

COMPLETENESS AND RELIABILITY OF RESPONSES

To gauge the completeness and reliability of responses, we considered several possible indicators:

- The language that most Salvadorans and Filipinos preferred to speak, on the presumption that, if the respondent did not speak and understand English well, more reliable data would probably be collected if the interview was conducted in the person's native language.

- Whether the interview was conducted in complete privacy or whether other persons were present who might have influenced the respondent's answers to the survey questions.

- The levels of item nonresponse, especially missing data on sensitive topics, such as immigration status, income, tax payments, and use of public services.

We also asked the interviewers to complete an "interviewer remarks" section at the end of each questionnaire to give us information about their perception of the respondent's overall reaction to the survey and his or her understanding of the questions. In addition, we debriefed interviewers at the end of the survey to get their perceptions of whether they thought respondents provided honest answers.

Language Used

Salvadoran respondents preferred to conduct the interview in Spanish, while the typical Filipino respondent opted to speak English. *All* of the Salvadoran interviews were completed in Spanish, while only 40 percent of the Filipino interviews were conducted in Tagalog. Anecdotal information we received from the field suggests that Filipino interviewers found it effective to use Tagalog to initially establish rapport with respondents but that once the interview began, the average respondent (as well as the interviewer) was generally more comfortable speaking in English. These experiences suggest that it is important to give the respondents the option of interview language, but it is also important, and often mandatory, that interviewers be bilingual.

These differences in language of interview correspond to respondents' answers to questions in the main interview about how well they could read, write, speak, and understand English at the time of the survey. In general, Filipino immigrants, both males and females, report being well versed in the English language across all dimensions. This is not surprising given the high level of education and types of occupations that Filipinos had before immigrating (see Chapter Five). Furthermore, English was the "official" language of instruction in the Philippines until the 1980s.

Among Salvadorans, men generally are more likely than women to report that they use the English language with a high degree of facility. Yet, just over half the men indicate that they understand English well (and only 25 percent report writing English well). The comparable figures for Salvadoran women are only 35 percent and 10 percent, respectively.

These results confirm the importance of not relying on English in interviewing Salvadoran immigrants, especially female respondents. On the other hand, English might have sufficed for the Filipino sample, given the nearly universal level of English competence among our respondents and their apparent preference (and that of the interviewers as well) for conducting "formal" business in English.

Privacy of Interviews

Fairly often, other family members were present at the time the interview was conducted, which may have influenced how respondents answered some sensitive survey questions. In 54 percent of the cases, others were present. In about 42 percent of these cases a spouse was present, 36 percent of the time there were children present, and in another 25 percent of the cases some other adult was present. There were no marked differences between Salvadorans and Filipinos. For both groups, others were more likely to be present if the respondent was female (58 percent of females had others present versus 50 percent of males). In comparison to other Los Angeles-based surveys conducted by RAND, the LACS was more likely to conduct interviews with spouses present. On a recent child-immunization survey that RAND conducted in Los Angeles County with about 800 Latino low-income residents, we found that spouses were present in only 16 percent of the interviews, compared with 42 percent for the LACS. One probable reason is that many Salvadoran and Filipino women were reluctant to be interviewed by male interviewers unless their spouses (or other relatives) were present.

Item Response/Nonresponse

As another indicator of the quality of the data collected in the LACS, we examine how often respondents did *not* answer the survey questions. Generally speaking, the level of item nonresponse (e.g., don't know, refused, no answer) is comparable to what is found on general population surveys. The rates are generally quite low, averaging under 5 percent for most items. Response rates were surprisingly high for the question about immigration status. There were a few questions, however, with higher-than-average item nonresponse: family income (which also generates a high rate of missing data on general population surveys) and amount of federal income taxes paid. Below we discuss response rates for these three items.

Immigration Status. Surprisingly, *all* respondents answered what we thought was the single most sensitive question—their current immigration status. In our pilot survey, we asked respondents to look at a card containing various immigration status options, including "without papers" (see Appendix C). Respondents were asked to tell the interviewer the number of the category on the card that best described their status. We purposely put this question near the end of the questionnaire so that it would be asked after the interviewer had had considerable time to establish rapport with the respondent.

These procedures seem to have worked. Furthermore, a number of respondents indicated that they entered the country illegally, and a considerable number acknowledged being undocumented immigrants at the time of the survey. Among our Salvadoran respondents, 89 percent indicated that they entered the United States without legal documentation. However, only 5 percent of the Filipinos in our sample indicated that they entered the United States as undocumented immigrants. Only 11 percent of Salvadorans said they entered as sanctioned immigrants (i.e., with a visa or as a resident). In contrast, our Filipino respondents primarily entered the United States on immigrant visas (70 percent). Another 21 percent entered the country on other types of visas.

Family Income. Respondents were first asked for their best estimate of total income from all sources for their family. Over 50 percent of respondents did not report an answer to this question.[15] Those who did not answer this question were then shown a card that listed 10 categories of income (see question G12 in Appendix B). As expected, over 70 percent of the respondents who did not provide an exact answer to the first income question did report an income category in response to question G12. In all, around 15 percent of respondents did not provide any income information (11 percent responded "don't know," and 4 percent refused). This nonresponse rate is generally comparable to that of other surveys inquiring about income.[16]

Salvadorans are less likely to report a family income than Filipinos are (80 percent compared with 86 percent), and, not surprisingly, the reported family incomes are much lower for the former than for the latter. This difference is consistent with the fact that Filipinos receive higher wages than Salvadorans and that they live in larger households that contain more workers on average.[17]

---

[15]Although the questionnaire allowed interviewers to distinguish nonresponses to this question into refusals or "don't knows," very few interviewers did so.

[16]In communications with survey directors at survey organizations throughout the country, we have found that the item nonresponse rate for nonsensitive questions is commonly in the 2–5 percent range, whereas comparable nonresponse rates for sensitive questions tends to be much higher, e.g., 8–11 percent for sexual behavior questions and 10–15 percent (or higher) for income questions. Income is generally considered by most respondents to be the single most sensitive question in household surveys.

[17]Filipino households contained an average of three persons who worked at least 15 hours per week, while Salvadorans had two "workers" per household, on average.

Tax Contributions. Perhaps no issue regarding immigrants has received more attention from the popular press and the general public than the question of whether immigrants contribute to the public coffers to pay for the publicly provided services that they use. Accordingly, we tried to collect information about the extent of tax contributions that these two immigrant communities make in Los Angeles. However, respondents had considerable difficulty answering these questions.

We asked respondents "Did you (or your husband/wife) file a federal income tax form for last year—that is, 1990?" (question G13). All but five respondents answered this question; 504 respondents answered affirmatively. Of those, however, only 200 were able to answer the next question (G14) about the amount of taxes paid; 277 reported that they did not know, and 24 refused to answer the question. We asked for the respondent's best guess of the federal income tax paid the previous year, but did not allow those unable to do so to then report a category, as we had with the income question.

For both Salvadorans and Filipinos, the percentage responding that they had filed a tax return generally increased with the permanency of their immigration status. These tax questions were among the most difficult for respondents to answer in our pilot study. We did not seek to verify the responses to these questions by looking at pay stubs or examining tax returns, but such procedures undoubtedly would improve reliability and validity in future studies.

Interviewer Perceptions of Data Quality

During our formal debriefing, interviewers reported that they believed respondents to have been extremely honest in their answers to questions about immigration status, with many freely admitting that they were undocumented immigrants at some time during their migration history. Some interviewers indicated that newly arrived immigrants were the most fearful about divulging answers to these questions, but they were generally cooperative and truthful in providing this information.

The interviewers also commented that most respondents were friendly and cooperative and tried to answer all questions to the best of their ability. However, many respondents had difficulty responding to some of the questions that asked about the entire household (e.g., family's income, expenses, use of public services). The respondents were generally comfortable providing answers about their own personal experiences but seemed to be a less reliable source of information about the entire family. Some questions, such as those inquiring into family members' use of public services and medical care, were especially difficult for respondents to answer because they often did not know the specific details of the type of service used or whether it was public or private, or the exact kind of insurance policies family members had. So a survey of immigrants may need to interview all members of the household regarding these issues if the aim is to develop reliable *family-level* estimates.

Interviewers also pointed out that respondents, after hearing the lists of possible services read to them in the health and public services portion of the survey, frequently requested more information about them. The field staff were uncomfortable that they did not have any type of handout with further information about public programs that might offer services to immigrant families. Survey staff should be able to provide information to respondents after the interview about available services and contacts as an additional benefit of participating in the survey.

After completing each survey, interviewers coded their impressions of the respondent's attitude toward the survey and how well he or she understood and responded to the questions. Our analysis of the interviewers' remarks shows that

- Sixty percent of the interviewers thought the respondents were very friendly and interested in the survey, whereas the rest were cooperative but not particularly interested. None of the respondents were perceived by interviewers as being "hostile."

- In the opinion of interviewers, 70 percent of respondents had a "good" understanding of the questions; only 3 percent were rated as "poor."

- Eighty-five percent of the respondents did not appear to have any significant problems answering the survey questions (e.g., no questions were confusing or angered the respondent). The remaining 15 percent mentioned problems with several "sensitive" items in the survey. The most frequently mentioned sensitive and personal questions were income, taxes, and expenses.

- For roughly 10 percent of the completed cases, interviewers indicated that they themselves found certain questions in the survey confusing or problematic (e.g., confusing skips, questions that were difficult to understand, etc.).

Chapter Five

CAN THE DATA COLLECTED INFORM POLICY?

The previous chapter examined the feasibility of implementing a representative survey of immigrants and of collecting reliable information about their behavior. We demonstrated that data presumed difficult to obtain—on immigration status, use of public services, and payment of taxes—can be collected reliably. The purpose of this chapter is to illustrate how data such as those we have collected can be used to inform important policy questions. In interpreting our results, the reader should keep in mind that they are only indicative and partial answers to the policy questions examined here. Our survey was a pilot: it is not representative of all immigrants, nor did we seek to address fully any one policy question.

Below we describe the information collected in the pilot study to suggest its usefulness in addressing four questions that are central to the current policy debate on immigration:

- How do groups of immigrants differ from one another?

- How does immigration status affect use of public services?

- How does immigration status affect payment of taxes?

- How does policy affect immigrant status?

IMMIGRANTS ARE NOT ALL THE SAME

In the current public and policy discourse, immigrants are often treated as an undifferentiated group with similar socioeconomic characteristics. At best, distinctions are made between undocumented immigrants and all other immigrants. Occasionally, distinctions are made between Hispanics and Asians. But rarely does the public and policy discourse recognize the extreme variations in socioeconomic characteristics between immigrants from different countries of origin, and even between immigrants from the same country of origin. Nevertheless, differences in socioeconomic characteristics between immigrants are important for public policy, for two reasons: (1) they determine the aggregate and distributional effects—both positive and negative—immigrants have on neighborhoods, localities, states, and the country as a whole, and (2) they can be affected significantly by policy, i.e., the congressionally established rules of eligibility for legal immigration can be changed, thus changing the nature of entering groups.

Our sample of Salvadoran and Filipino immigrants provides a powerful illustration of how immigrants can differ significantly from one another in socio-demographic characteristics, immigration status at entry and reasons for entry, role in the labor market, and demand for public services.

Socio-Demographic Characteristics

The most significant difference between the two groups of immigrants is in their level of schooling and their mastery of English. As shown in Table 5.1, nearly one in two Salvadorans has six years or less of schooling, almost none have even one year of college, and a majority do not understand or read English well. By contrast, more than two out of three Filipino immigrants have some college, and nearly all understand and read English well. As we will see later, most Filipinos had acquired their education and learned English before entering the United States.

Salvadoran immigrants are also younger than their Filipino counterparts. This difference is explained in part by the fact that immigration from El Salvador to the United States began more recently than immigration from the Philippines, our ally during World War II. One out of three Salvadorans has been in the country for ten years or more, compared to two out of three Filipino immigrants (Table 5.1). In both groups of immigrants, females outnumber males (55 versus 45 percent) and married

Table 5.1

Socio-Demographic Characteristics of Salvadoran and Filipino Immigrants

Characteristics	Salvadoran Immigrants	Filipino Immigrants
Education		
Six years or less (%)	44	14
Some college (%)	3	70
Median years of schooling	7	15
Language (%)		
Understand English well	42	97
Read English well	33	95
Age (%)		
18–29	47	19
50–64	6	28
Gender (%)		
Female	55	54
Marital status (%)		
Married	62	75
Spouse absent	3	15
Never married	28	19
Time in the United States		
Ten years or more (%)	26	56
Median years	7	12

immigrants outnumber singles at least two to one.[1] In nearly all cases, spouses are residing in the United States with their partners, regardless of immigration status. There are no differences in this pattern between Salvadoran and Filipino immigrants.

Immigration Status at Entry

Nearly all Salvadoran immigrants in our sample (90 percent) initially entered as undocumented immigrants. The pattern is reversed for Filipino immigrants: only one out of twenty entered the country illegally, and three out of four entered as legal permanent immigrants (Table 5.2).

While the forms of entry differ between the two immigrant subgroups, their predominant reasons for coming to the United States do not. Both sought enhanced economic opportunities. Family reunification is the second most frequent reason for Filipino immigrants, but it is a reason for only one out of ten Salvadoran immigrants. The second most frequent reason for Salvadoran immigrants is fear for personal safety. That reason was given by one out of four immigrants.

Wages and Roles in the Labor Market

Because of their higher levels of education and English proficiency, Filipino immigrants command higher wages than Salvadoran immigrants do—twice as high for males and even more than that for females (Table 5.3). The *family* income of Filipino families is more than four times higher than the income of Salvadoran families, because Filipino households are larger (see Table 4.3) and contain more workers.

Table 5.2

Status at Entry: Salvadoran and Filipino Immigrants

At Entry	Salvadoran Immigrants	Filipino Immigrants
Immigration status		
Undocumented	89%	5%
Permanent resident	4	72
Other[a]	7	22
Reasons for entry		
Family reunification	12	45
Enhanced opportunities	57	51
Safety reasons	26	1
Other	5	3

[a]Includes various types of temporary visas, including student and tourist visas.

---

[1]As noted in the previous chapter, our respondents were more likely to be married than the general Salvadoran and Filipino immigrant population residing in Los Angeles County (62 versus 48 percent and 75 versus 62 percent, respectively).

Table 5.3

Labor Market Characteristics: Salvadoran and Filipino Immigrants

Labor Market Characteristics	Salvadoran Immigrants	Filipino Immigrants
Weekly wages (median $)		
Male	238	500
Female	175	400
Income ($)		
Median family income	11,484	47,323
Percent employed		
Male	80	85
Female	69	78
Occupations (%)		
Male		
Managerial/professional/technical support	5	21
Administrative support	1	24
Precision product/craft	46	13
Assemblers/laborers	27	20
Private household service	0	0
Female		
Managerial/professional/technical support	5	31
Administrative support	1	32
Precision product/craft	12	7
Assemblers/laborers	12	7
Private household service	42	1

Differences in human capital are also reflected in differences in labor force participation and in occupational structure. Filipino immigrants are slightly more likely to be employed than Salvadoran immigrants. The differences are larger among females than among males.

With regard to occupational structure, the two subgroups of immigrants display reverse images. Whereas nearly one out of two male Filipino immigrants and over three in five female Filipino immigrants work in managerial, professional, technical, or administrative support occupations, only 6 percent of both male and female Salvadoran immigrants are found in these occupations. Salvadoran males are primarily craftsmen, assemblers, and laborers. Salvadoran women—two out of five—are disproportionately employed in private household services.

Satisfaction With Life in the United States

In spite of their large differences in education, income, and experience of life in the United States, the two subgroups of immigrants agree on one thing: they are overwhelmingly satisfied with life in the United States (Table 5.4). And Salvadoran immigrants were no more likely to feel overwhelmed by the day-to-day difficulties they may encounter. However, the stresses of life do take a greater toll on Salvadoran immigrants than on their higher-income Filipino counterparts. Salvadorans are somewhat more likely to report they "felt nervous and stressed" very to fairly often in the 30 days preceding the interview (24 versus 15 percent).

Table 5.4

Attitudes Towards Life in the United States: Salvadoran and Filipino Immigrants

Attitudes	Salvadoran Immigrants	Filipino Immigrants
Respondent "completely" to "fairly" satisfied with life in the United States now	89%	93%
Respondent felt difficulties were piling up so high he/she could not overcome them "very" or "fairly" often in the past thirty days	16	12
Respondent felt nervous and stressed "very" or "fairly" often in the past thirty days	24	15

USE OF PUBLIC SERVICES AND IMMIGRATION STATUS

Little systematic information is available about how immigrants of varying status make use of the broad range of public and other services available to them. Such information is needed not only for planning purposes at all levels of government but to address reliably the question of the costs immigrants may impose on local and state governments. This question is particularly salient for undocumented immigrants.

We asked our survey respondents whether they or anyone in their family had used a broad array of public and private services at least once over the past twelve months. The services included fell into four categories: income transfer and nutrition programs, health services, special purpose services (e.g., libraries and public transport), and education. Below, we examine how immigration status within each immigrant group affects service use. Overall, our pilot results suggest that the use of public services is generally not affected by immigration status, including undocumented status. The results suggest, and our multivariate analyses confirm,[2] that the main factors affecting the use of transfer programs and health services are income and number of children, most particularly children age five or under. In addition, the use of special services is affected by factors influencing the need for the service in the first place, such as number of children, English proficiency, or desire to change immigration status.

Transfer Programs

The relatively high income of Filipino immigrants renders them ineligible for income-tested programs such as AFDC, general relief, and food stamps. In contrast, one in ten Salvadoran immigrant families received AFDC at least once in the past year, one in five received food stamps, and one in three benefited from the Women, Infants, and Children (WIC) program, a special supplemental food program that provides food, vitamins, counseling, and health care referrals to pregnant women

---

[2]See Appendix E for the results of our multivariate analyses.

and to children under the age of five (Table 5.5). In addition to income, the number of children under the age of five is a major determinant of use of the WIC program.

There are some variations in the use of transfer programs by immigration status, but these are consistent with differentials in income between the various subgroups of immigrants. Although undocumented immigrants are not eligible for AFDC and food stamps, they benefited indirectly from these programs through either their eligible citizen children or their eligible relatives. Indeed, there is growing evidence that immigrant families contain members with different immigration status, ranging from undocumented to temporary, permanent, and naturalized citizens.[3]

Both subgroups of immigrants seem to benefit equally from unemployment compensation. But Salvadoran immigrants are twice as likely as Filipino immigrants to receive worker's compensation, possibly a reflection of their differential occupational structure. Unemployment and worker's compensation are workplace related, and their use seems to be independent of immigration status or income.

Health Services

Just as Salvadoran immigrants are more likely than Filipino immigrants to use income support programs, they also are more likely—nearly three times more likely—to rely on public hospitals and on county and free clinics for their health care needs (Table 5.6). The corollary is that they are less likely to use private doctors or clinics and three times less likely to be enrolled in a health maintenance organization (HMO). Finally, and consistent with their lower incomes, they are also three times less likely to have seen a private dentist at least once in the year preceding the inter-

Table 5.5

Use of Transfer Programs by Immigration Status: Salvadoran and Filipino Immigrants

Transfer Programs	Salvadoran Immigrants					Filipino Immigrants		
	Undocu-mented	TPS[a]	Temporary Visa	Permanent Resident	All	Permanent Resident	Citizen	All
AFDC	14%	10%	13%	6%	9%	2%	1%	1%
Food stamps	22	17	18	14	17	4	1	2
WIC	33	28	34	20	26	6	0	2
Unemployment compensation	8	8	8	10	9	13	8	10
Worker's compensation	4	6	0	8	6	3	3	3
Average annual income (dollars)	10,250	10,800	11,250	13,000	11,485	37,630	50,000	47,325

[a]TPS means Temporary Protective Status.

[3]For instance, see Comprehensive Adult Student Assessment Systems (CASAS), *A Survey of Newly Legalized Persons in California*, San Diego, 1989.

Table 5.6

Use of Health Services by Immigration Status: Salvadoran and Filipino Immigrants

Health Services	Salvadoran Immigrants					Filipino Immigrants		
	Undocu-mented	TPS[a]	Temporary Visa	Permanent Resident	All	Permanent Resident	Citizen	All
Public hospital	30%	24%	29%	21%	25%	10%	10%	10%
County, free, or family clinics	52	50	53	35	45	16	10	12
Prenatal clinics	17	20	16	14	16	6	4	4
Private doctor or clinic	31	48	39	51	45	52	62	58
HMO	8	13	8	21	15	38	51	47
Private dentist	7	25	18	28	22	61	75	69
Immunization	42	48	53	43	45	28	18	23
Average annual income (dollars)	10,250	10,800	11,250	13,000		37,630	50,000	

[a]TPS means Temporary Protective Status.

view. Their equally low use of public dentists suggests that Salvadoran immigrants may be deferring their dental care.

The pattern of use of public versus private health services appears to be unrelated to immigration status. Undocumented immigrants are as likely, if not more likely, to use public hospitals or county and free clinics than their counterparts with temporary or permanent visas. Whatever differences are observable are generally consistent with differences in income.

Undocumented immigrants, however, are less likely than their counterparts with legal status to use private doctors and clinics as well as HMOs and private dentists. One potential reason for this pattern may be found in the pattern of government versus private insurance coverage. Table 5.7 shows that health insurance coverage in general and private health insurance in particular are associated with income. It also suggests that undocumented immigrants are much less likely to be covered by private insurance or an HMO.

Our multivariate analyses suggest that other factors also affect the pattern of public health service use and government health insurance coverage noted above. Higher public service use and likelihood of government coverage are associated with the number of children below age 5 and the presence of adults age 65 or over. Females are also more likely to use public hospitals and to be covered by government health insurance.

Other Services

Because a greater proportion of Salvadorans have had to seek adjustments to their previously undocumented or temporary status, they were more likely to have used legal services than their Filipino counterparts (Table 5.8). On the other hand, the use

Table 5.7

Health Insurance Coverage by Immigration Status: Salvadoran and Filipino Immigrants

| Insurance Coverage | Salvadoran Immigrants | | | | | Filipino Immigrants | | |
	Undocu- mented	TPS[a]	Temporary Visa	Permanent Resident	All	Permanent Resident	Citizen	All
Any health insurance	39%	40%	37%	44%	41%	87%	90%	88%
Government program	35	28	32	22	28	26	26	26
Private insurance	3	7	11	15	10	56	58	57
HMO	7	10	3	18	12	40	53	49
Payer								
Employer/union[b]	6	10	11	19	14	77	83	81
Privately purchased	0	0	3	2	2	7	5	6
Average annual income (dollars)	10,250	10,800	11,250	13,000		37,630	50,000	

[a]TPS means Temporary Protective Status.
[b]Paid by either respondent or respondent's spouse.

Table 5.8

Use of Selected Services by Immigration Status: Salvadoran and Filipino Immigrants

| Service | Salvadoran Immigrants | | | | | Filipino Immigrants | | |
	Undocu- mented	TPS[a]	Temporary Visa	Permanent Resident	All	Permanent Resident	Citizen	All
Legal services	14%	24%	34%	11%	17%	4%	1%	2%
Public transport	70	61	66	60	63	25	28	26
Recreation	52	46	37	58	52	62	71	66
Libraries	21	22	32	32	28	47	71	62

[a]TPS means Temporary Protective Status.

of public transportation seemed to be independent of immigration status. Salvadorans were much more likely to have used public transportation than Filipino immigrants were.

Libraries and public parks are the only two services that Filipino family members had used more frequently than Salvadoran immigrant family members. The number of children age 6–17 rather than immigration status seemed to be a major determinant of use of these two services. In addition, greater English proficiency and attendance in U.S. schools led to greater use of public libraries.

In our survey, we also asked about use of a number of support services in addition to those discussed above: VD programs, rape crisis services, protective services for children, women's shelters, programs to pay utilities or rent, senior citizen centers, and counseling. Utilization of these services was extremely low by both subgroups of immigrants—typically less than 1 percent of respondent families.

Education

Education is the single costliest service provided to natives and immigrants alike. Table 5.9 provides a one-point-in-time glance at the number of children in school at the time of our survey in 1991. It also shows the extent to which adult immigrants of different immigration status used English as a second language (ESL) classes, and educational and vocational training services since they entered the country.

Salvadoran immigrants had slightly fewer children in schools at the time of the survey than Filipino immigrants, possibly because they are typically younger. Among Salvadorans, the number of children in school per family with children of school age varied little regardless of immigration status: i.e., families of undocumented immigrants had the same average number of children in school, 1.6 per family, as permanent legal immigrants. But because undocumented immigrants were more likely to be single than permanent immigrants (27 versus 17 percent), the number of children in school per undocumented respondent was lower than for permanent residents.

In interpreting these figures, the reader should keep in mind that the various subgroups differentiated here by country of origin and immigration status are at different stages in their lives and in the time they have spent in the United States. Large disparities among immigrants at one point in time may not be maintained through their lives.

The extent to which children attend public or private schools appears to depend both on income and on immigration status. The children of Salvadoran immigrants

Table 5.9

Use of Education by Immigration Status: Salvadoran and Filipino Immigrants

Education	Salvadoran Immigrants					Filipino Immigrants		
	Undocu- mented	TPS[a]	Temporary Visa	Permanent Resident	All	Permanent Resident	Citizen	All
Children								
Number of children in school per family with children in school	1.57	1.68	1.37	1.58	1.57	1.68	1.89	1.83
Number of children in school per respondent[b]	0.24	0.47	0.29	0.59	0.45	0.41	0.86	0.69
School attended								
Public	100%	100%	100%	93%	95%	85%	76%	78%
Private or parochial	0	0	0	7	5	15	24	22
Adults								
Ever attended school in U.S.	21%	20%	16%	36%	26%	12%	32%	24%
Adult education classes	12	13	13	19	15	0	4	3
Secondary schools	8	6	3	12	8	5	6	5
Some college or more	1	—	—	3	1	7	22	16
Ever attended vocational training	7	6	16	13	10	21	34	28
Ever attended ESL classes	45	57	55	82	64	6	9	8

[a]TPS means Temporary Protective Status.

[b]Includes all respondents regardless of marital status or whether or not they have children.

attended public schools exclusively. The only exception is for a small percentage of children (7 percent) of Salvadoran permanent immigrants. In contrast, from one out of six to one out of four school-age children of Filipino immigrants attended private or parochial schools.

By and large, school attendance in the United States by adult immigrants is relatively low. Salvadoran permanent immigrants and Filipino naturalized citizens had the highest incidence of school attendance; one out of three reported having attended some school in the United States. Attendance in school by all other adult immigrants in our study did not exceed one out of five. Undocumented adult immigrants were as likely as persons of other immigration status to have attended school.

Salvadoran immigrants who attended schools in the United States did so for different purposes than Filipino immigrants. The majority of Salvadorans attended adult education classes or secondary schools. In contrast, Filipino immigrants who attended schools in the United States primarily went to college, reflecting their higher education levels and English proficiency at entry.

Just as Filipino immigrants were more likely to have attended college in the United States, they were also more likely to have received vocational training. One in three naturalized citizens and one in five permanent immigrants did so. Reflecting their lower levels of education and English proficiency, Salvadoran immigrants were much less likely to have received vocational training in the United States, regardless of immigration status. However, permanent residents as well as immigrants on temporary visas were twice as likely to have received vocational training than their undocumented counterparts and the holders of Temporary Protective Status.

For those who attended vocational training, the type of training sought did not differ significantly between Salvadoran and Filipino immigrants. Nearly two out of three got training for one of the following three activities: secretarial/business, computer/electronics, and medical assistant/nursing.

Finally, the differentials in English proficiency at entry between the two subgroups of immigrants are dramatically reflected in their attendance of ESL classes. Nearly half of the undocumented Salvadoran immigrants at one time attended ESL classes, whereas more than four out of five permanent Salvadoran immigrants had done so by the time of their interview. In contrast, less than one in ten Filipino immigrants attended ESL classes.

TAX FILINGS AND PAYMENTS AND IMMIGRATION STATUS

To fully assess the net public costs or benefits of international immigration, detailed and comprehensive information is needed on the incidence of tax payments by immigrants, in addition to comprehensive information on their use of public services. A full account of tax contributions requires obtaining information on payments by immigrants for all forms of taxes, including income, excise, sales, property, and business taxes. For the purpose of our pilot survey, we focused on obtaining information on income tax payments. We also sought information on expenditure patterns and mortgage and rental payments, which would form the basis for computing sales and property tax payments. As noted earlier, we were generally successful in obtaining such data from most respondents.

Table 5.10 shows the incidence of tax filings and payroll tax deductions for Salvadoran and Filipino immigrants, by immigration status. It suggests that federal income tax filing is highly dependent on immigration status. Less than 40 percent of undocumented immigrants reported filing federal tax returns in the year before the interview (1990). Permanent legal immigrants reported the highest incidence of federal income tax filings, 85 percent or more. Salvadoran permanent immigrants were somewhat less likely than their Filipino counterparts to have filed tax returns. Temporary immigrants' filings of federal tax returns fell in between those two extremes.

We also asked about actual amounts of income taxes paid. As noted earlier, many respondents were unable to provide this information—not because they did not want to (only 5 percent of Filipino respondents and 3 percent of Salvadoran respondents refused to answer the question), but because they did not know from memory. Future surveys will need to ask to see copies of tax returns in order to obtain this information more comprehensively.

Failure to file a federal tax return generally translates into nonpayment of income taxes. As shown on Table 5.10, the proportion of all respondents who filed a federal tax return *or* had federal taxes deducted from their paychecks is similar to the proportion of all respondents who filed federal tax returns. This suggests that those who have taxes deducted from their paychecks also file tax returns.

Table 5.10

Federal Tax Filings and Payroll Deductions by Immigration Status: Salvadoran and Filipino Immigrants

Tax Filings and Payroll Deductions	Salvadoran Immigrants					Filipino Immigrants		
	Undocumented	TPS[a]	Temporary Visa	Permanent Resident	All	Permanent Resident	Citizen	All
Filed federal taxes[b]	38%	54%	63%	84%	64%	91%	95%	93%
Filed federal tax or reported payroll tax deductions	38	55	63	84	64	92	96	94
Payroll deductions[c]								
Any	50	52	53	72	60	97	96	97
Federal taxes	46	51	37	72	57	94	96	95
State taxes	50	49	40	72	57	94	96	95
Social Security	46	51	44	70	57	91	91	91
Health insurance	9	6	12	25	15	47	62	52
Average annual income (dollars)	10,250	10,800	11,250	13,000	11,567	37,630	50,000	42,083

[a]TPS means Temporary Protective Status.
[b]Percent of all respondents.
[c]Percent of respondents who worked the week preceding the interview.

POLICY AFFECTS IMMIGRATION STATUS

As noted above, nearly all our Salvadoran respondents had entered the country without inspections, i.e., illegally. But by the time they were interviewed, on the average 7.6 years later, only one out of four remained undocumented (Figure 5.1). All others had been legalized as a result of two recent federal policy initiatives: two out of three were amnestied under the Immigration and Control Act of 1986 (IRCA). The others had applied and were approved for Temporary Protective Status: included in the Immigration Act of 1990, this new category allows undocumented immigrants (and asylum seekers whose applications have been denied) from a designated country to remain in the United States temporarily until conditions in that country improve. Holders of this status are protected from deportation and are authorized to work in the United States.

Few of the Filipinos had entered the country illegally and, as expected, even fewer remained in this status at time of interview. But a significant proportion, one out of four, reported entering the country on a visitor or other temporary visa. Overstaying the duration of a temporary visa is another significant means of "illegal" entry into the United States. By the time they were interviewed, on the average 12.5 years later, nearly all those who had entered on a temporary visa had been adjusted to permanent immigrant status by qualifying through either the family reunification or employment-based categories.

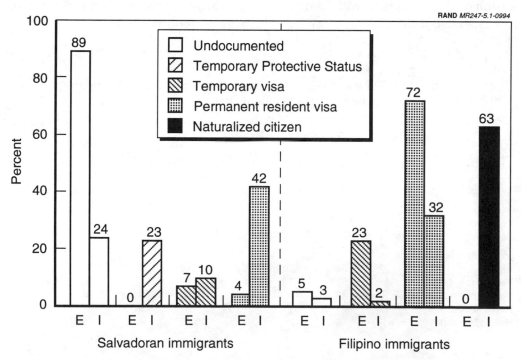

NOTE: E means status at entry in the country and I means status at time of interview in summer/fall of 1991.

Figure 5.1—Changes in Immigration Status for Salvadoran and Filipino Immigrants

Another change of immigration status is drawing growing policy attention: the extent to which permanent immigrants avail themselves of their rights to become naturalized citizens of the United States. For many, this gesture is viewed as one measure of an immigrant's integration into the nation's socio-political culture. Our Filipino respondents shed some light on this issue. Nearly two out of three had become naturalized citizens of the United States by the time of our interview, on the average about 12.4 years after their entry into the country. Eighty-five percent of the remaining immigrants said they intended eventually to become citizens.

Generally, our Salvadoran immigrants had not been in the country long enough to be eligible for naturalization. But half indicated that they intended to become citizens, with another 25 percent indicating they "did not know." This pattern held regardless of immigration status.

CONCLUSIONS

In this chapter we have illustrated that data collected from immigrants about their immigration status, socio-demographic characteristics, labor market behavior, use of public services, and tax payments can be used to address critical policy questions and inform the public debate on immigration and immigrant policies. Although the data await empirical confirmation from a larger sample of immigrants from more countries of origin, we have reached several tentative conclusions that have important potential policy implications. The first conclusion is that the relative success of immigrants in the labor market and their demand for a broad range of public income-transfer, nutritional, health, and special-purpose programs depend in large measure on their education and English proficiency when they enter this country. The policy implication is that immigration's effects on the economy and on demand for public services are shaped in the first place by the criteria used to determine eligibility for immigration into the United States.

A second conclusion is that U.S. laws offer many alternative avenues for undocumented immigrants to become legal permanent immigrants—whether they have entered without inspection or with a temporary visa that they have overstayed. Access to these avenues may actually encourage illegal immigration, since they offer the opportunity for undocumented immigrants to jump ahead of the queue of people seeking entry as resident immigrants. This suggests that undocumented and legal immigration are not independent flows, and that a desire to decrease the size of one may require decreasing (or increasing) the size of the other. Finally, and to the extent that the legal status of "undocumented" is a temporary status soon to be adjusted to permanent legal immigrant, what is the purpose of denying these people access to such basic services as education and preventive health care, as some legislative proposals are now contemplating? Today's undocumented worker may be tomorrow's permanent resident.

A third conclusion is that the use of public services has less to do with people's immigration status and more to do with relative income, family size, and other factors that determine their needs. At one level this is not surprising, since our public service delivery system at all levels of government has a predominant redistributive function. Even undocumented immigrants indirectly benefit, through eligible children or relatives, from income-transfer and other programs for which they themselves are not directly eligible.

Finally, and in contrast to the above, the filing of federal tax returns and the incidence of payroll tax deductions appear to be very much related to immigration status. We found that undocumented immigrants were the least likely to file returns or to have their taxes deducted from payroll; permanent legal immigrants were the most likely to file tax returns, with temporary immigrants falling in between these two groups. The implications of the previous and this last conclusion are threefold. One is that the net public costs of immigrants depend very much on their socio-demographic characteristics at entry. The second is that the costs of providing public services will vary among immigrants, just as they vary among natives. Finally, there appears to be a cost in the form of lost public revenues associated with undocumented and temporary statuses.

Chapter Six

BENEFITS AND FEASIBILITY OF A NATIONAL IMMIGRANT SURVEY: LESSONS FROM THE LACS

There are a number of lessons to be learned from the experience of designing and fielding the LACS and analyzing the resulting data. In this chapter we summarize the evidence that such a survey can provide the data needed to answer critical immigrant policy questions, and we present the lessons learned that can be of use to those who would plan and conduct a national immigrant survey.

THE KINDS OF POLICY QUESTIONS SURVEY DATA CAN ANSWER

The results of the LACS clearly indicate that such surveys can give policymakers the kinds of data they need to develop immigration and immigrant policy. The large differences between the Salvadoran and Filipino communities in the LACS indicate that "immigrants" are not a homogeneous lot; they are, rather, composed of diverse groups. The substantial differences among them on many dimensions must be considered in policymaking because policies could affect groups differently and could thus have unforeseen (and possibly undesirable) political, social, and economic effects.

To illustrate these points, we return to some of the basic questions raised in Chapter Two and see how the LACS results can address them for the groups we studied.

Assimilation of Immigrants

We begin with questions related to social and economic integration:

- Are immigrants becoming culturally and economically integrated into mainstream America?

- How do immigrants move into better-paying, more stable jobs? What factors should policies emphasize: vocational training, formal education, learning English, personal contacts, or changing immigration status?

On these dimensions, Salvadorans and Filipinos have very different experiences and (related) characteristics. The average Filipino has a family income more than four times higher than the average Salvadoran. Filipino workers had higher weekly wages (in 1991 dollars) on their first jobs (despite the fact that Filipinos have, on average, been in the United States longer) and higher weekly earnings on their most recent jobs.

What accounts for these differences—or, put in terms of the questions, what should policies emphasize? The greatest differences between the two groups are in education and mastery of English. Filipinos not only enter the country with more education, but once they are here they are as likely as Salvadorans to get some further formal education, and they are nearly three times as likely to obtain vocational training. Almost all Filipinos in the sample can understand, speak, read, and write English well, whereas the majority of Salvadorans do not have good English skills. Salvadoran women are especially unlikely to know English well: only a third report that they understand English well, and only 10 percent report that they can write it well.

These disparities in education and English proficiency translate into very different occupational structures: more than half the Filipinos work in managerial, professional, technical, or administrative support jobs, compared to less than 10 percent of Salvadorans. The latter are primarily craftsmen, assemblers, and laborers.

The "Costs" of Immigration

Among the most highly charged immigrant issues is whether immigrants "pay their way" or are a net drain on society. Two of the policy questions are related to these issues:

- Do immigrants use public support strictly to get on their feet, or do they become dependent on it?

- What fiscal burden does immigration create?

Before policymakers can address the first question and its policy implications, they need to know what kinds of public services immigrant groups use. Nearly all Salvadoran respondents with school-age children had those children in public schools. In contrast, a fourth of Filipinos with school-age children sent them to private or parochial schools. In general, Salvadoran immigrants made much greater use of public services, including income-transfer and nutritional programs and health services. Indeed, the only services that Filipino immigrants used more heavily were libraries and public parks. We were also able to obtain information on service use by immigration status, including "undocumented." Our data suggest that use of public services has less to do with people's immigration status and more to do with relative income, family size, and other factors that determine needs.

Use of public services by immigrants raises concern in some quarters about the economic burden immigrants create—especially given uncertainty about how much they contribute in taxes. The LACS results indicate that surveys can collect data on this issue. Tax filing depended very much on immigration status. Only two in five undocumented immigrants reported filing federal taxes in the year preceding the interview, compared to more than half of immigrants on temporary status and more than 80 percent of permanent residents. (These figures were similar for both groups.) Payroll tax deductions are similarly dependent on immigration status. Among undocumented respondents who worked the week preceding the interview, 50 percent had their federal and state taxes deducted, compared with 72 percent of Salvadoran permanent residents and 97 percent of Filipino permanent residents.

Policies and Immigrant Status

A final question is how policy affects immigrant status. Many in the sample who were permanent residents had originally entered on a visitor or other temporary visa. Overstaying the duration of such a temporary visa is another significant means of "illegal" entry into the United States. By the time of the survey, nearly all who had entered using such visas had become permanent residents, qualifying through either the family reunification or employment-based categories.

The dynamic pattern of adjustments from undocumented or temporary visa to permanent immigration status raises a critical issue that has not been addressed in the debate over ways to discourage undocumented immigration: how much does increasing legislated options available for these adjustments actually encourage further illegal immigration? For many, these options may just be a means for would-be permanent immigrants to jump ahead of the queue.

This question needs further empirical analysis, with a more representative sample of immigrants. If these options do have that effect, there are two important policy implications. First, undocumented and legal permanent immigration are not independent flows, and reducing one may require reducing the other. Second, the distinction between undocumented and permanent immigrant is an important legal construct. But it may have questionable validity from a social perspective—most notably in the case of denying access to education and preventive health care. There seems little purpose in denying access to a person who, although undocumented today, will be eligible tomorrow.

LESSONS THAT MAY GUIDE A NATIONAL SURVEY OF IMMIGRANTS

Besides showing that immigrant surveys can provide critical policy-relevant data, the LACS also provides strong evidence that a national survey is feasible. It suggests important lessons about survey design and procedures and about the types of data that can and should be collected.

Assessment of Pilot Survey Procedures

The survey procedures developed for the Los Angeles Community Survey of Salvadoran and Filipino immigrants were largely successful, and they provide encouraging evidence for the feasibility of conducting future longitudinal surveys of immigrants.

- Once a residential address or eligible immigrant family was contacted, the response rates were quite good—around 65 percent of those with whom we made some contact for the screener and 70 percent for the main interview. These are somewhat better than we expected, considering that schedule and cost constraints prevented us from implementing additional procedures that probably would have boosted the participation rates by at least ten percentage points (such as increasing the number of callbacks, attempting refusal conversions, tracking people who moved, etc.).

• Most of the nonresponse was due to locating problems (locked or security buildings, or people who could not be reached within four callbacks) rather than refusals to participate. Refusal rates were quite low (about 9 percent).

• Immigrant families were remarkably cooperative and willing, in most cases, to divulge sensitive information about themselves, including their immigration status and information that would permit follow-up in a longitudinal survey. Among Salvadorans, 90 percent indicated entering the country without proper documentation. Furthermore, over 80 percent of the Salvadoran and Filipino respondents interviewed provided their names and telephone numbers to permit possible survey follow-ups.

• We were successful in recruiting, training, and retaining a large, highly educated bilingual interviewing staff (about 35 interviewers) throughout the bulk of the 10-week field period. With a few exceptions, we were pleased with the overall quality of the interviewers' work.

— The interviewers were highly motivated and committed to the research;

— They were comfortable working in high-crime areas;

— They were effective in persuading most respondents to participate at both the screener and main interview phase;

— By standard survey measures, most performed their interviewing job quite well. Their productivity rates were generally high, refusal rates were low, and missing data problems were minimal.

With respect to the pilot survey costs, the total cost per complete case, counting the screening and main interview phase, was roughly $545 per interview (total data collection costs divided by the number of completed main interviews). This includes data collection and processing costs, as well as field management and pretesting costs. As expected, this cost is somewhat greater than the estimated $400 to $500 cost per completed interview reported for a one-hour interview in English in surveys of the general population.[1] These figures, however, do not include costs of survey design.

We learned a great deal from the pilot study about the similarities and differences in conducting general population surveys and immigrant surveys. On balance, the similarities far outweigh the differences (when one compares studies of similar scope and complexity that are conducted in inner cities). All complex personal-interview

---

[1]Personal communications with survey professionals of other research institutions conducting large-scale longitudinal surveys.

studies that require large, primarily new, interviewing staffs face similar challenges. The most common problems are the following:

- Finding enough qualified interviewer applicants, particularly if special skills/ characteristics, such as bilingualism, are needed.

- Finding local residents who are willing to work in high-crime inner cities.

- Keeping interviewers motivated to complete their assignments.

- Mounting effective community outreach activities to solicit support for the survey from community leaders and local residents.

- Designing effective training programs for complicated questionnaires and complex field procedures.

- Hiring a sufficient number of experienced supervisors.

- Implementing appropriate quality control checks, especially for new staff, throughout the fieldwork to gauge interviewer performance and data quality.[2]

Despite the similarities, we found in the course of conducting the pilot survey that there were some unique aspects of an immigrant survey that make the data collection management tasks (recruitment, training, supervision, and quality control) considerably more complicated and time-consuming to implement successfully. The management issues and problems at each stage of the survey process, starting with instrument design and pretesting, were especially difficult and challenging for the senior staff and for the junior members of the team.

We think that the optimal approach to recruiting, training, and supervising a large multicultural interviewing team is to use a multicultural (and experienced) supervisory team to carry out these activities. However, we found it especially difficult to locate suitable Filipino staff. Although it was fairly easy for us to find a Spanish-speaking supervisor with survey research experience, it was virtually impossible to find a comparable Tagalog-speaking supervisor. Throughout the pilot the project team was far more confident about our ability to supervise and maintain appropriate quality control over the Spanish-speaking interviewers because we had the bilingual supervisor as a member of the core survey team. The fact that we did not have a Filipino supervisor (or experienced Filipino interviewer) on the management team was a major drawback in our ability to confidently supervise the Tagalog-speaking interviewers and gauge how well they were really performing in the field (when they interviewed in Tagalog). It would have been preferable to increase the overall level of interviewer supervision (and validation), using experienced bilingual staff, particularly during the early stages of the fieldwork, to collect more systematic data about interviewers' performance and to give more direct feedback to the staff on how to improve their basic interviewing skills.

---

[2]For an excellent discussion of current standards and practical procedures for designing and implementing surveys, see Fowler (1988).

The management problems mentioned above are particularly severe when dealing with multiple cultural groups within a single survey. In our case, the requirement for both Spanish-speaking and Tagalog-speaking interviewers increased the management problems by a significant factor.

Recommendations for Survey Procedures

In some ways, the pilot results provide conservative indicators of the likely success of future immigrant surveys. Budget and time constraints prevented us from implementing many field procedures that probably would have improved the overall response rates and the data quality. The pilot results, however, lead us to conclude that future surveys of immigrants, including longitudinal surveys, can be successfully designed and implemented. Below we discuss several critical research issues that must be addressed to ensure the success of future surveys of immigrant populations.

1. Identifying a probability sample of immigrants. While the pilot demonstrated that it is possible to draw a representative sample of immigrants using census data on where immigrants are concentrated, there is a serious potential pitfall in the process that must be avoided to ensure the success of the sampling procedures. It is crucial to list and screen all addresses in target areas, especially many hidden apartment units that may not be easily visible from the street and are likely to house one or more immigrant families. We found that the field lister for the pilot (who was not bilingual) failed to properly list a substantial proportion of the apartments in the high-density Salvadoran census tracts. We suspect that this occurred in part because the field lister was not entirely comfortable working in many of the high-crime areas and that he failed to fully investigate hidden units because of legitimate concerns about his personal safety and language barriers. Interviewers found that the "hidden" apartment units missed by the original lister often contained undocumented immigrants. This means that failure to properly list addresses for immigrant samples can lead to an undercount of immigrants, and especially those who are undocumented.

To minimize these listing problems on future surveys, we have three recommendations:

* Use a team of bilingual field interviewers who are comfortable working in the areas to complete both the listing activities and the actual screening and interviewing.

* Validate a random percentage of each lister's work to ensure the accuracy of the listings before the actual fieldwork begins.

* Provide adequate training for interviewers on field listing so that they can identify potential listing problems when they are in the field and bring them to the attention of the field supervisor.

2. Developing and testing questionnaires suitable for administration with different immigrant groups. A major lesson learned from the pilot is that the design and testing of effective instruments in several languages (in our case, English, Spanish, and Tagalog) is time-consuming and requires close collaboration between the design team, the translators, and outside consultants and informants.

To design effective translated instruments for different language groups, we suggest that the following elements be included in the survey design process:

- The designers should consider translatability of measures during the early stages of instrument design, so that the English and non-English questionnaires are developed in parallel.

- All survey instruments should be pretested extensively in all languages with respondents from the target groups.

- Iterative pretests should be conducted on individual questions or sections of the questionnaire that have never been used with the study population or are particularly problematic.

- Multiple pretesting methods should be used as appropriate, including focus groups and one-on-one pretests.

- There should be as many pretests as are necessary to ensure that all problematic questions have been corrected.

- Bilingual interviewers who are representative of the immigrant populations that will be included in the study should conduct the testing of translated instruments.

- Bilingual members of the survey design team should attend some of the pretest interviews, to observe the interviewer-respondent interactions as the translated instruments are being tested in the field.

- Highly skilled translators with a proven track record, familiarity with the study population(s) and the spoken language they use, and acquaintance with survey research should be hired to work closely with the survey team during the design and testing process and during the preparation of the final version of all survey materials.

As a further test of how well the final instruments actually work in the field, we also recommend that a random percentage of main interviews be observed by a bilingual field supervisor (this step could be incorporated into field validation) to monitor respondent reaction to the translated instruments. It would also be useful to collect systematic data from interviewers about their perceptions of how well the translated instruments really worked. Results from both these steps would improve researchers' understanding of whether the translated instruments meet the design objective.

3. Recruiting and retaining a high-quality bilingual field staff. Without a highly skilled and committed bilingual field interviewing staff, surveys of immigrant populations whose first language is not English cannot be successfully implemented. The pilot interviewers' effectiveness in interacting with immigrants and reassuring them about the confidentiality of the survey and the importance of their participation was a critical factor in the success of the field operations. Our ability to successfully recruit and retain a large bilingual staff throughout the field period (a five-week screener plus a five-week main interview phase) rested on four key elements:

- We identified a qualified pool of bilingual interviewers from the same immigrant groups that were included in the study.

- We conducted extensive training sessions on the background and purpose of the study, aggressively solicited feedback from interviewers about their concerns, and gave them an opportunity to ask questions until they were comfortable with the project and their role as interviewers.

- The interviewers saw themselves as members of the research team and were dedicated to making the project a success: they were convinced that the survey might have a future positive effect on the Salvadoran and Filipino communities.

- Interviewers were convinced that RAND's confidentiality assurances were real and that they were not putting the respondents at risk.

Interviewer concerns about RAND's promises of confidentiality and our willingness to deliver on those promises were a major topic during training. They needed assurances about confidentiality issues before they were willing to approach respondents. To give added confidence to potential interviewers and respondents about the researchers' commitment to data safeguarding, we strongly recommend that future studies apply for a Department of Health and Human Services (DHHS) confidentiality certificate that will guarantee that individual data will be protected from subpoena. We did not have such a confidentiality certificate for the pilot study, but past RAND survey experiences suggest that it is an especially effective device for persuading interviewers and respondents that the privacy of survey data will be securely protected.[3]

Successful recruitment of bilingual interviewers requires several other components. One critical item is the selection of competitive pay rates (and incentive payments) that will permit the survey staff to attract and retain high-quality field interviewers. While we were successful during the pilot using a pay rate of $7.50 per hour (plus a modest $2.00 bonus per completed case for the main interviews) in attracting high-quality field interviewers, most survey organizations have found it necessary to offer substantially higher pay rates (in the $8–$10 per hour range), often coupled with large incentive payments (e.g., high per-case bonuses for completed interviews) in order to recruit (and retain) interviewers who are willing to work in high-crime areas. After 10 weeks of working in difficult areas, there were signs that the LACS interviewers were beginning to burn out on the job. We suspect that substantially more attractive incentives would have been necessary had the field period been much longer.

---

[3]To protect the confidentiality of our respondents, we did not keep permanent records of information that would allow any of them to be identified.

The second critical component for effective interviewer recruitment and retention is to assure their safety in the field. This can be done by providing escorts or survey assistants, or by allowing interviewers to work in teams if they prefer. We were fortunate during the pilot that the overwhelming majority of our interviewers (who were primarily male) were comfortable working in high-crime areas in Los Angeles County, and such precautions were not necessary. It is unusual to have so many male interviewers in a general survey, and even more surprising to find so many interviewers willing to work under less than optimal field conditions. We were also fortunate that our pilot sample was highly clustered, so many interviewers were frequently working in the same general area. They felt considerable comfort in knowing that their colleagues were often close by. If the fieldwork is less clustered or if female interviewers are required, interviewers are more likely to have legitimate safety concerns, which may affect their willingness to work by themselves or to persist with the work for long periods.

Another interviewer safety concern may arise regarding respondent payments. Our interviewers were extremely uncomfortable carrying cash, so we opted for grocery certificates.

4. Obtaining high survey participation and retention rates. The ultimate success of future surveys obviously depends on obtaining high response rates and retention rates among immigrants. Besides some of the measures already discussed, we think that future efforts to maximize response rates should include the following additional components:

- *Appropriate incentive payments.* We found that a $5.00 grocery certificate (in lieu of cash) was an effective, but administratively burdensome, incentive payment; future studies might want to test whether larger incentive payments, say $10.00, would help to boost response rates.

- *Innovative procedures for gaining access to locked/security buildings when apartment managers refuse to allow interviewers to enter* (e.g., special letters and phone calls from senior project staff or community leaders to solicit cooperation). Apartment building gatekeepers appear to be a major problem in surveying immigrants in some densely populated areas.

- *Tracking highly mobile immigrant groups.* We found that 11 percent of the Salvadoran sample had moved within a period of 4–6 weeks, but most respondents were willing to provide at least partial tracking information during the screener to facilitate future longitudinal follow-ups, though postcards provided for this purpose in our pilot were rarely sent by the respondents who did move.

5. Designing effective field management procedures. Managing field operations for a large-scale immigrant survey, especially one that includes multiple language groups, poses several unique challenges for the survey management team because of (1) the need for bilingual field supervisors (as well as interviewers), (2) the need to recruit and train a large field staff of typically inexperienced interviewers for whom English is their second language, and (3) the need to screen large samples of households to identify eligible respondents.

In planning future immigrant surveys, we recommend that the following elements be included in the field management plans:

- Recruit bilingual supervisors and validators so that the supervisory staff is sufficiently large to monitor the quality of interviewers' work.

- Use a mixed mode approach to randomly validate a percentage of each interviewer's work[4] (e.g., in-person and telephone validation), do so quickly, and give direct ongoing feedback to interviewers on the results of the validation.

- Edit and code incoming completed cases on an ongoing basis to pinpoint interviewer errors as soon as possible and give direct feedback to interviewers on the results of the editing.

- Conduct in-home observations for a random percentage of all interviewers' work to judge their performance as well as respondent reaction to the translated instrument.

- Organize activities so that supervisors can maintain frequent personal contact (e.g., weekly meetings) with interviewers throughout the survey period.

- Provide ongoing opportunities for the entire staff to meet in groups to share information about their experiences and concerns.

Effective field management of immigrant surveys requires supervisors to establish a good working relationship with the bilingual interviewers, one in which they are comfortable talking about their experiences—both negative and positive. The supervisors must be perceived as sensitive and responsive to the cultural differences and concerns of the interviewers. Good communication channels between the supervisory staff and the field interviewers are, therefore, essential to the successful implementation of any future surveys of immigrants.

The Need for Longitudinal and Family-Member Data

The LACS collected data on a number of different topics and found that immigrants are generally able and willing to report information about themselves, including such sensitive topics such as their immigration status. Collection of this information was undoubtedly facilitated by the assurances of confidentiality and the use of show cards, which kept the respondents from having to state outright their income or immigration status. Also, we put these questions near the end of the questionnaire so that they would come after the interviewer had had some time to establish a rapport with the respondent.

1. **Data on changes over time.** The survey also demonstrated the feasibility of collecting retrospective data from immigrants regarding, for example, their work and earnings before coming to the United States, when they first arrived in the country,

---

[4]We found that our interviewers-to-supervisor ratio was inadequate during the pilot (one supervisor was responsible for 14–21 interviewers) and that we could not monitor the new interviewers' work as closely as desired.

and their immigration status upon entry. For example, all but nine respondents were willing and able to provide information on what they earned on their first job in the United States. Such information can be valuable for studying the adjustments of immigrants and the changes that they experience (see, for example, Greenwell, DaVanzo, and Valdez, 1993). On some dimensions, retrospective data can provide a readily available, less-expensive substitute for longitudinal data. The experience of the LACS suggests that we could probably have collected even more retrospective information, e.g., date of marriage.

There are a number of topics, however, that are crucial for studying immigrants' adjustments—e.g., attitudes, assistance received from friends and relatives, or service use—that probably cannot be reported retrospectively. Furthermore, a one-time cross-sectional survey will cover only those currently in the United States and will not include those who have returned to the home country. With a longitudinal survey, those in the country at the baseline interview are sought for reinterview at a later date. Hence, the original sample may include some who have returned to their home country by the time of the follow-up interview and whose baseline characteristics can be analyzed and compared to the characteristics of those who remained in the United States (although it is not clear whether these individuals can easily be distinguished from respondents who cannot be reinterviewed for other reasons, e.g., those who moved to a different residence within the sample area).

Retrospective and longitudinal data each have their strengths and weaknesses. On the one hand, the former are less expensive to collect, there is no risk of being unable to reinterview respondents to collect data on the more recent period, and a long period of time can be covered. On the other hand, there are questions about respondents' ability to report on past events, including some topics that are particularly relevant for studying immigrants' adjustments to life in the United States, and about the quality of those reports. Ideally one would use a combination of the two approaches. Even in a longitudinal study, it is useful to know about respondents' experiences before the baseline survey.

2. Data on other family members. While respondents to the LACS seemed to have few problems reporting on their own characteristics and experiences, even for the past, they found it considerably more difficult to report on other members of their household. This may be due in part to the fact that immigrants tend to live in larger households than the native-born do and are generally more likely to live in extended households. Based on the experience of the LACS, we would recommend that other household members be interviewed directly if it is important to collect information about them or about their children. For items asking about the entire household, or other topics where the respondents may not know the precise answer, e.g., household expenses or amount of taxes paid, it is important to allow for reports in broader categories. Although we thought it would be more time-consuming, it appears that information about household composition and the characteristics of various household members would probably have been collected more easily if we had used a household roster listing all members of the household, rather than collecting information on groups of them (e.g., number of children in a particular age group, number of workers).

CONCLUSIONS

There are, of course, real differences in size, duration, and cost between our pilot study and a national survey. Even so, the LACS demonstrates that a survey designed specifically to provide useful data on immigrant families and their adaptation processes, though challenging and expensive, is indeed feasible.

A new study of the type we propose would require a great deal of time, money, and expertise. Major investments are required in the personnel, advanced planning, and surveillance needed to conduct a survey in immigrant neighborhoods. Bilingual interviewers and immigrant respondents require considerable time to complete interview tasks with which other populations may already be familiar. Addressing ethical concerns about privacy and confidentiality may require more time than is often taken in the course of current survey research efforts, as may allowing for culturally appropriate behavior. As a result of these factors, LACS interviewers spent close to four hours per completed case to locate respondents and conduct a one-hour interview. This does not include the time for interviewer training or field supervision.

A rough cost estimate based on our experience in Los Angeles suggests that preparing and conducting the initial interview for a survey of 9,000 immigrants in nine sites across the country would cost about $6 million. (This assumes that the survey would be conducted in six high-density and three low-density urban areas, focusing on selected groups of immigrants in each location.) Costs for subsequent years would vary considerably. For a panel survey, they would depend mainly on tracking effort: how much time would be spent locating respondents who had moved since the last interview. For a cross-sectional design, screening costs—driven by the difficulty of identifying each new qualifying household—would be the key variable. In any event, survey costs would be substantial. But they would surely be low compared to the potential costs that immigration may impose, or even to the costs of programs intended to address immigration issues.

For policymakers seeking to understand the effects of immigration on society, even the most extensive survey is no panacea. The issues are so complex, and the concerns and relationships so varied, that no single effort can resolve them all. But at every level, the public debate *does* need new data. Understanding the economic and social effects of immigration policy means understanding how immigrants adapt to life in the United States. Only a large, specially designed survey can provide this understanding. By directly examining the changes and adjustments in the adaptation process, a new survey can give policymakers the facts they need to face the challenges of unprecedented immigration.

SCREENER QUESTIONNAIRE

INTERVIEWER QUESTION AND ANSWER SHEET FOR THE LOS ANGELES COMMUNITY SURVEY

SCREENER INTERVIEW

IF THE RESPONDENT ASKS YOU MAY SAY THE FOLLOWING ABOUT:

WHAT IS THE "LOS ANGELES COMMUNITY SURVEY?"

This is a survey of Los Angeles residents to learn more about how families from other countries adjust to living and working in Los Angeles. We're currently conducting a short five minute personal interview with a sample of approximately 6000 households located throughout Los Angeles County. We plan to do another more extensive interview with a sample of 600 families later this summer.

WHO IS DOING THIS STUDY?

The study is being carried out by RAND, which is a private, non-profit public policy research organization located in Santa Monica, California. RAND conducts research on many different topics such as health care, education and work training, housing for low income families, and many other topics of interest to members of the general public.

We are NOT conducting this survey for the Immigration and Nationalization Service (INS), OR the Police, OR any Social Service Agency. This is a scientific research study and we are not part of any form of law enforcement. Your participation in this survey is voluntary and will not affect any services your household needs or uses from any local or federal program.

WHO IS SPONSORING THE STUDY?

This study is sponsored by a grant from the Ford Foundation. The Ford Foundation was incorporated in 1936 (by Henry Ford). Its purpose is to advance public well-being by identifying and contributing to the solution of problems of national and international importance. In addition to public policy research, the foundation also supports programs in the areas of human rights, education and culture, community service, and foreign affairs.

HOW DO I KNOW YOU'RE NOT FROM THE POLICE OR IMMIGRATION SERVICE?

I am a professional interviewer from RAND and I have an identification card with my picture, a letter from the RAND researchers who are conducting this study, and a Question and Answer Pamphlet that describes this study. SHOW RESPONDENT THESE MATERIALS.

If you like, you can also call my supervisor at RAND--her name is _____ and ask for more information about this study. HAND CARD WITH SUPERVISOR NAME AND PHONE NUMBER. There is a supervisor on duty at RAND who can speak to you in English or (Spanish/Tagalog).

WHY WAS MY HOUSEHOLD SELECTED?

Your household was selected at random. We used information from the 1980 census to select a random sample of neighborhoods throughout Los Angeles County--including Carson, Long Beach, Hollywood, Silverlake, Pico-Union, and others areas in LA. In each neighborhood, we're visiting every household on the block and asking them to complete a short five minute survey. We are asking a total of about 6,000 families to take part in this study.

WHAT WILL HOUSEHOLDS BE ASKED TO DO?

All households in your neighborhood will be asked to participate in a short interview. We will ask a few questions about you and your household, like the language the people here usually speak at home, how old each person is and where he or she was born. This interview takes about 5 minutes and any adult in the household can answer these questions.

2

In some cases, you or a member of your household may be invited to participate in another interview later this summer about your family's experiences living and working in Los Angeles. That interview will be conducted with families in your neighborhood in about one month. But you don't have to make a decision about that now--if you're selected to participate in the second part of this survey, we'll schedule an appointment to explain the study in detail and you can decide later whether or not you'd like to participate in the second interview.

DO I HAVE TO ANSWER?

Your participation is voluntary, but I hope that you will decide to participate in this important research study. Once you begin the interview, if there is a specific question you don't want to answer, that's OK. You can stop the interview at any time. We need and appreciate any information you do provide.

WHAT HAPPENS TO THE INFORMATION?

We will combine your answers with answers from everyone else who took part and report the results as totals, averages, summaries, and other general statistics for the entire group. This information will be used for research purposes only. We will keep all information about your identity private. This means that your name or address will not appear in any reports resulting from this interview.

IF R HAS FURTHER QUESTIONS ABOUT CONFIDENTIALITY, SAY:

I am sorry that I couldn't answer your questions, but I'd be happy to have my supervisor at RAND, _____, talk to you about this. She can answer any questions or concerns you may have about your participation. I can have her call you, or--if you prefer--you can call her collect at RAND. GIVE RAND CARD WITH SUPERVISOR NAME AND PHONE NUMBER.

WHY SHOULD I PARTICIPATE?

Your responses to this survey may play a role in planning programs and policies that help families-- from other countries--adjust to living and working in California.

This is a special opportunity to be part of an important scientific study. Only you can provide the information that we need. By participating in this survey, you can make a valuable contribution to a study that may help plan future programs and services for members of your community.

This is one of a only a few scientific studies examining how people adjust to life in Los Angeles after they move here from other countries. Because we're surveying a scientifically selected sample of people to participate, we need to include many different kinds of people--people just like you--in order to have a better understanding of the views and experiences of people who live in Los Angeles.

IF RESPONDENT WANTS MORE DETAILS ABOUT THE "SECOND INTERVIEW," YOU MAY SAY THE FOLLOWING ABOUT:

- WHEN WILL THE INTERVIEW TAKE PLACE?
  I don't know the exact time but it will probably take place sometime this summer. I'd like to find out what days and times are generally good for you so that we can recontact you to schedule a convenient time to explain the study and see if you'd be willing to participate.

- HOW LONG IS THE SECOND INTERVIEW?
  I don't know the exact time--but it's probably about 45 minutes. When we recontact you the interviewer will explain how long the interview will take and exactly what you'll be asked to do. Then you can decide if you want to participate.

3

- **WILL I BE PAID?**
  If you decide to participate in the second interview, RAND will give you a $5.00 certificate to use at your local grocery store--to show our appreciation for your participation in this important research study.

- **WHY ARE YOU INTERESTED IN TALKING WITH PEOPLE FROM EL SALVADOR, THE PHILIPPINES, AND OTHER CENTRAL AMERICAN COUNTRIES?**
  We're inviting about 600 people who were born in one of eight different countries in Asia or Latin America to tell us more about their families' experiences living and working in Los Angeles and about special concerns and needs that families had trying to adjust to life in Los Angeles.

  We want to collect information that will help us better understand the problems and issues that families face adjusting to life in Los Angeles after they move here from other countries. A large proportion of families who have settled in Los Angeles County come from Asian and Latin American countries. Therefore the RAND researchers decided that this particular survey would focus on people who were born in the Philippines, El Salvador, and other Central American countries. In future work, other groups may be included. We did not have enough money for this particular study to include ALL families in the survey.

- **WHAT GOOD WILL IT DO?**
  It will increase our understanding about the special problems and issues that families face in adjusting to life in California. And it will provide decisionmakers with accurate information--that is not currently available--about the characteristics of families and the kinds of problems and experiences that they have when they move to Los Angeles. It will also help identify the special public programs and services that are used and needed by these families.

- **WHY DO YOU NEED TO SELECT A PARTICULAR PERSON FROM THE HOUSEHOLD TO PARTICIPATE IN THE SECOND INTERVIEW?**
  For the purposes of this study, we need to interview an adult between the ages of 18 and 64 who was born in (ELIGIBLE COUNTRIES).

  In some cases more than one Adult in a household may be eligible, so we interview the person with the most recent birthday. This ensures that every eligible person in the household has an equal chance of being selected.

  We need to make sure that we represent the views of all people--young and old, men and women, people who are heads of households and people who are not. By selecting one person from the household at random we can do this.

WHY CAN'T SOMEONE ELSE ANSWER FOR SELECTED RESPONDENT?

We will be asking some questions about how people feel about their OWN personal experiences, so only they can really answer those questions.

IF R HAS FURTHER QUESTIONS THAT YOU CANNOT ANSWER, SAY:

I am sorry that I couldn't answer your questions but I'd be happy to have my supervisor at RAND, _____, talk to you about this. She can answer any questions or concerns you may have about your participation. I can have her call you, or--if you prefer--you can call her collect at RAND. GIVE RESPONDENT A CARD WITH THE SUPERVISOR'S NAME AND PHONE NUMBER. BE SURE TO WRITE YOUR INTERVIEWER NAME AND ID ON THE CARD BEFORE LEAVING.

RAND
1700 Main Street, P.O. Box 2138
Santa Monica, CA 90407-2138

Rev. 5/16/91

LOS ANGELES COMMUNITY SURVEY
HOUSEHOLD SCREENING FORM

CARD 01   7-8/

CASE ID LABEL   1-6/

FORM TYPE: **S C**   9-10/

A. FINAL STATUS:

COMPLETE	1	11/
BREAKOFF	2	
REFUSAL	3	
LANGUAGE BARRIER	4	
(Which?_____)		12-13/
ILLNESS/SENILITY	5	
INACCESSIBLE	6	
VACANY	7	
BUSINESS ADDRESS	8	
OTHER (SPECIFY)_____	9	
		14-15/

B. INTERVIEW CONDUCTED IN:

ENGLISH (YELLOW FORM)	1	16/
SPANISH (GREEN FORM)	2	
TAGALOG (BLUE FORM)	3	
OTHER_____	4	
(What?_____)		17-18/
NO INTERVIEW	5	

C. TOTAL CALLS: ☐☐   19-20/

D. LENGTH OF INTERVIEW: ☐☐ Minutes   21-22/

E. ELIGIBILITY STATUS:

NO ELIGIBLE R AT ADDRESS	0	23/
R FROM BELIZE	1
R FROM COSTA RICA	2
R FROM EL SALVADOR	3
R FROM GUATEMALA	4
R FROM HONDURAS	5
R FROM NICARAGUA	6
R FROM PANAMA	7
R FROM THE PHILIPPINES	8
UNKNOWN	9

F. LANGUAGE USUALLY SPOKEN BY HH MEMBERS:

UNKNOWN	0	24/
ENGLISH	1
SPANISH	2
TAGALOG	3
ILOCANO	4
OTHER_____	5
(What?_____)		25-26/

G. INTERVIEWER'S NAME & ID: ☐☐☐☐   27-30/

H. DATE CASE FINALIZED: ☐☐ / ☐☐ / **9 1**   31-36/
MONTH   DAY   YEAR

1

INTRODUCTION TO SCREENER INTERVIEW

Hello, my name is _____. I'm from RAND, a research organization in Santa Monica. (SHOW RAND IDENTIFICATION CARD AND INTRODUCTORY LETTER). ASK TO SPEAK TO AN ADULT HOUSEHOLD MEMBER.

How would you prefer that I speak with you:

In English, *or*

SPANISH: O ¿si usted prefiere, en Español?

TAGALOG: Kung gusto mo ay sa Tagalog.

We're conducting a survey about how families from other countries adjust to life in Los Angeles. These questions will only take about 5 minutes, and the interview is completely voluntary. We would like you to help us today by answering a few questions about the people who live in your household, like the language the people in this household usually speak at home, how old each person is and where he or she was born.

I'd like to begin the interview now if it is OK with you -- it will only take 5 minutes.

A. Could you tell me what language the people in your household usually speak at home?   RECORD INFORMATION IN ITEM F ON COVER OF SCREENER.

LANGUAGE HH USUALLY SPEAKS
_____

- IF R HAS QUESTIONS, USE SUGGESTED ANSWERS ON THE "QUESTION AND ANSWER SHEET."

- IF ADULT IS NOT AVAILABLE, SCHEDULE AN APPOINTMENT AND RECORD ON CASE RECORD FOLDER.

- IF R REFUSES OR BREAKS OFF THE INTERVIEW, COMPLETE THE REFUSAL/BREAKOFF FORM.

2

1. First, I have some questions about all the people who live in this (house/apartment). Think about all the people who usually live here--adults, children and babies. Don't count people who are on active military duty, or living away at school or college, or who sleep somewhere else most of the time.

Including yourself, how many people live here?

INTERVIEWER RECORD TIME STARTED:

☐ ☐ : ☐ ☐   37-40/

AM 1   41/
PM 2

NUMBER OF
HOUSEHOLD MEMBERS: ☐ ☐   42-43/

2. Were you or any of the people who live in this (house/apartment) born outside the United States?

(Circle One)

YES .... 1 ---> | ANSWER A | 44/

NO--ALL HOUSEHOLD MEMBERS
WERE BORN IN THE U.S. .... 2 ---> | GO TO Q.13, PAGE 7 |

A. HAND CARD TO R. Were you or any of the people who live in this (house/apartment) born in any of the countries listed on this card?

IF YES, ASK: Which ones?

NO .... 0 ---> | GO TO Q.13, PAGE 7 | 45/

(OR)

| SHOW |
| CARD |
| A |

YES, FROM: *(Circle All That Apply)*

BELIZE 1   46/
COSTA RICA 2   47/
EL SALVADOR 3   48/
GUATEMALA 4   49/ GO TO Q.3, NEXT PAGE
HONDURAS 5   50/
NICARAGUA 6   51/
PANAMA 7   52/
THE PHILIPPINES 8   53/

CARD 01

3. I need to ask a few more questions about you and the people who live in your (house/apartment). First let's start with you, could you give me your first name, your age, and where you were born?

Next, I'd like to list the same information about all other adults and children who live here. Please tell me the first name of the people who live here, their ages, and where each person was born. FILL IN HH ROSTER, STARTING WITH INFORMANT.

- DO NOT INCLUDE PEOPLE WHO ARE AWAY ON ACTIVE MILITARY DUTY, LIVING AT SCHOOL, OR PEOPLE IN JAIL OR OTHER INSTITUTIONS.
- DO INCLUDE PEOPLE AWAY TEMPORARILY--ON VACATION, IN THE HOSPITAL FOR A FIXED STAY, ETC.
- BE SURE TO PROBE FOR ALL HOUSEHOLD MEMBERS.

Country Codes List

Belize	01	Nicaragua	06
Costa Rica	02	Panama	07
El Salvador	03	The Philippines	08
Guatemala	04	U.S.	09
Honduras	05	Other	10

3. FIRST NAME ONLY	4. SEX — IF NECESSARY, ASK: Is (NAME) male or female?	5. AGE ON LAST BIRTHDAY	6. COUNTRY OF ORIGIN — If other, what?
INFORMANT: 01. _____ 54/	Male ...... 1 55/ Female 2	AGE: 56–57/	COUNTRY CODE: 58–59/ 60–61/
OTHER HH MEMBERS: 02. _____ 62/	Male ...... 1 63/ Female 2	AGE: 64–65/	COUNTRY CODE: 66–67/ 68–69/
(REPEAT 4-6 FOR EACH HH MEMBER) 03. _____ 70/	Male ...... 1 71/ Female 2	AGE: 72–73/	COUNTRY CODE: 74–75/ 76–77/
04. _____ 9/	Male ...... 1 10/ Female 2	AGE: 11–12/	COUNTRY CODE: 13–14/ 15–16/ (CARD 02) 7–8/ 1–6/
05. _____ 17/	Male ...... 1 18/ Female 2	AGE: 19–20/	COUNTRY CODE: 21–22/ 23–24/
06. _____ 25/	Male ...... 1 26/ Female 2	AGE: 27–28/	COUNTRY CODE: 29–30/ 31–32/
07. _____ 33/	Male ...... 1 34/ Female 2	AGE: 35–36/	COUNTRY CODE: 37–38/ 39–40/
08. _____ 41/	Male ...... 1 42/ Female 2	AGE: 43–44/	COUNTRY CODE: 45–46/ 47–48/
09. _____ 49/	Male ...... 1 50/ Female 2	AGE: 51–52/	COUNTRY CODE: 53–54/ 55–56/
10. _____ 57/	Male ...... 1 58/ Female 2	AGE: 59–60/	COUNTRY CODE: 61–62/ 63–64/

CARD 01 / 02

7. Just to be sure, is there anyone else who <u>usually</u> lives here that you haven't told me about--including babies and small children?

(Circle One)

YES .... 1 —> ENTER NAME IN ROSTER, ASK Q.3-Q.6

NO .... 2 —> CONTINUE WITH Q.8

65/

8. INTERVIEWER CHECK ROSTER TO DETERMINE IF HOUSEHOLD IS ELIGIBLE FOR MAIN INTERVIEW:

HOW MANY HOUSEHOLD MEMBERS ARE AGE 18-64 (AND) BORN IN EITHER EL SALVADOR (OR) THE PHILIPPINES?

(Circle One)

NONE .... 0 —> CONTINUE WITH Q.9

ONE .... 1 —> GO TO Q.10, NEXT PAGE

TWO OR MORE .... 2 —> GO TO Q.11, NEXT PAGE

66/

9. IF NO HH MEMBER BORN IN EL SALVADOR OR THE PHILIPPINES, FOLLOW INSTRUCTIONS BELOW:

9A. INTERVIEWER CHECK ROSTER:

WERE ANY HH MEMBERS AGE 18-64 BORN IN THE FOLLOWING SIX CENTRAL AMERICAN COUNTRIES?

ELIGIBLE COUNTRIES:
Belize
Costa Rica
Guatemala
Honduras
Nicaragua
Panama

(Circle One)

YES .... 1 —> ANSWER Q.9B

NO .... 2 —> GO TO Q.13, PAGE 7

67/

9B. IF YES TO Q.9A, SAY: We're especially interested in talking with people who were born in other countries. You or someone else in your household may be asked to participate in another interview about your experiences living and working in Los Angeles. That interview will be conducted in about one month. Just in case you or someone else in your household is selected to participate in the second part of this study, I'd like to find out the best time to reach you so I can schedule an appointment to explain the study and see if your household would be willing to participate.   RECORD BEST TIME TO CALL BACK ON CASE RECORD FOLDER.

* ASK INFORMANT FOR HIS/HER FIRST AND LAST NAME SO WE CAN RECONTACT HIM/HER *

( ) CHECK HERE AND FILL OUT RECONTACT FORM ON PAGE 6.

CARD 02

CARD 02

THIS PAGE FOR HH MEMBERS BORN IN EL SALVADOR OR THE PHILIPPINES:

10.   ONE ELIGIBLE HOUSEHOLD MEMBER BORN IN EL SALVADOR OR THE PHILIPPINES, SAY:

We're especially interested in talking with people who were born in other countries. I'd like to invite (ELIGIBLE RESPONDENT), to participate in a second interview--in about one month--to answer more questions about your families' experiences living and working in Los Angeles. Could you tell me (ELIGIBLE RESPONDENTS) first and last name? Is (ELIGIBLE RESPONDENT) here now? I'd like to find out the best time to reach (you/him/her) so I can schedule an appointment to explain this study and see if (you/he/she) would be able to participate in another interview in about one month.   RECORD BEST TIME TO CALL BACK ON CASE RECORD FOLDER.

RECORD NAME OF ELIGIBLE R ON CASE RECORD FOLDER AND ENTER   Line No. on Roster:
PERSON'S LINE NUMBER FROM THE ROSTER IN THESE BOXES: ⟶   68-69/

( ) CHECK HERE AND FILL OUT RECONTACT FORM ON PAGE 6.

11.   MORE THAN ONE ELIGIBLE HOUSEHOLD MEMBER BORN IN EL SALVADOR OR THE PHILIPPINES, SAY:

11A.   We're especially interested in talking with people who were born in other countries.   To be sure I talk to the right person, can you tell me which of these people (READ NAMES OF ELIGIBLE HH MEMBERS), had the most recent birthday?

RECORD NAME OF ELIGIBLE R ON CASE RECORD FOLDER AND ENTER   Line No. on Roster:
PERSON'S LINE NUMBER FROM THE ROSTER IN THESE BOXES: ⟶   70-71/

11B.   I'd like to invite (ELIGIBLE RESPONDENT) to participate in a second interview--in about one month--to answer more questions about your families' experiences living and working in Los Angeles. Could you tell me (ELIGIBLE RESPONDENTS) first and last names? Is (ELIGIBLE RESPONDENT) here now? I'd like to find out the best time to reach (you/him/her) so I can schedule an appointment to explain this study and see if (you/he/she) would be able to participate in another interview in about one month.   RECORD BEST TIME TO CALL BACK ON CASE RECORD FOLDER.

( ) CHECK HERE AND FILL OUT RECONTACT FORM ON PAGE 6.

RECONTACT FORM FOR ELIGIBLE HOUSEHOLDS ONLY
(El Salvador/Philippines/Other Eligible Central American Country)

12. In case you have moved or we can't locate you when we come back to do the interview (in about a month), may I have the names, addresses, and telephone numbers of three people who would know how to locate you? For example, this could be your parents, a grandparent, an aunt or uncle, some other relative, or a friend—anyone you're sure to keep in touch with. (ASK R TO LOOK UP ADDRESS, PHONE NUMBER.)

INTERVIEWER CHECK:

ENTER NUMBER OF CONTACTS GIVEN:		72/
NONE - REFUSED INFORMATION	......	0
ONE NAME	......	1
TWO NAMES	......	2
THREE NAMES	......	3

A.

Last Name _____ First _____

Street Address _____

City _____ State _____ Zip _____

(___) _____
Area Code   Telephone

What is this person's relationship to you? (For example, mother, father, grandmother, aunt, sister, friend, etc.)

_____
Person's Relationship to You

B.

Last Name _____ First _____

Street Address _____

City _____ State _____ Zip _____

(___) _____
Area Code   Telephone

What is this person's relationship to you? (For example, mother, father, grandmother, aunt, sister, friend, etc.)

_____
Person's Relationship to You

C.

Last Name _____ First _____

Street Address _____

City _____ State _____ Zip _____

(___) _____
Area Code   Telephone

What is this person's relationship to you? (For example, mother, father, grandmother, aunt, sister, friend, etc.)

_____
Person's Relationship to You

THANK R AND REMIND HIM/HER THAT A RAND INTERVIEWER (WILL/MAY) RECONTACT HIM/HER IN ABOUT ONE MONTH. LEAVE COPY OF QUESTION AND ANSWER SHEET.

(GO TO Q.13 NEXT PAGE)

7

FOR EVERYONE:

(CARD 03)   7-8/

1-6/

13. That's the end of this interview. I just need to ask two final questions for our recordkeeping.

   A. Is there a telephone at this residence where you can be reached?

      (Circle One)

        YES 1   9/

        NO 2

14. Just in case my office wants to make sure I was here to do this interview, what is your telephone number?

Area Code   Telephone

    (OR)

    REFUSED .... R   10/

Thank you for participating in this important study. We really appreciate your help.

IF ELIGIBLE HOUSEHOLD: REMEMBER TO LEAVE A COPY OF THE RAND QUESTION AND ANSWER SHEET AND THE CHANGE OF ADDRESS CARD AND REMIND INFORMANT THAT AN INTERVIEWER WILL RECONTACT (SELECTED RESPONDENT) IN ABOUT ONE MONTH.

INTERVIEWER RECORD TIME ENDED:

    ☐☐ : ☐☐   11-14/

    AM 1   15/

    PM 2

CARD 03

1

INTRODUCTION TO SCREENER INTERVIEW

Buenos días (buenas tardes/buenas noches). Me llamo (FIRST, LAST) y represento a la organización RAND, un centro de investigación en Santa Monica. (SHOW RAND IDENTIFICATION CARD AND INTRODUCTORY LETTER). ASK TO SPEAK TO AN ADULT HOUSEHOLD MEMBER.

¿Como prefiere que la hable, en inglés,...

SPANISH: O en español?

TAGALOG: Kung gusto mo ay sa Tagalog.

RAND esta llevando a cabo una encuesta sobre como las familias que vienen de otros paises, se adaptan a las condiciones de vida en Los Angeles. Estas preguntas sólo tomarán (5) minutos y la entrevista es completamente voluntaria. Quisiéramos que nos ayude a contestar unas cuantas preguntas acerca de las personas que viven en esta casa, por ejemplo, como que idioma hablan generalmente en casa, la edad de cada persona que vive en esta casa, y donde nacieron él o ella.

Quisiera empezar la entrevista, (si le parece)--solo tomará 5 minutos.

A.   ¿Podría decirme que idioma se habla generalmente en esta casa?   RECORD INFORMATION IN ITEM F ON COVER OF SCREENER.

LANGUAGE HH USUALLY SPEAKS

- IF R HAS QUESTIONS, USE SUGGESTED ANSWERS ON THE "QUESTION AND ANSWER SHEET."
- IF ADULT IS NOT AVAILABLE, SCHEDULE AN APPOINTMENT AND RECORD ON CASE RECORD FOLDER.
- IF R REFUSES OR BREAKS OFF THE INTERVIEW, COMPLETE THE REFUSAL/BREAKOFF FORM.

2

INTERVIEWER RECORD TIME STARTED: 37-40/

⏱   [ ][ ] : [ ][ ]

AM 1   41/

PM 2

1. Primero, tengo unas preguntas relacionadas con todas las personas que viven en (esta casa/este apartamento). Piense en todas las personas que _por lo general_ viven aquí -- adultos, niños y criaturas. No incluya a las personas que están haciendo su servicio militar, o a las que van a la escuela o universidad y no viven en (esta casa/este apartamento), o a las que duermen la mayor parte del tiempo en otro sitio.

¿Incluyendolo/Incluyendola a usted, cuántas personas
viven aquí?

NUMBER OF
HOUSEHOLD MEMBERS: [ ][ ]   42-43/

2. ¿Nació usted, o nació cualquier otra persona que vive en (esta casa/este apartamento), en _otro_ país que los Estados Unidos de
Norteamérica?

(Circle One)

YES .... 1 --->   ANSWER A   44/

NO--ALL HOUSEHOLD MEMBERS
WERE BORN IN THE U.S. .... 2 --->   GO TO Q.13, PAGE 7

A. HAND CARD TO R. ¿Nació usted, o nació cualquier otra persona que vive en (esta casa/este apartamento) en uno de los países que
figuran en esta tarjeta?

IF YES, ASK: ¿En cuáles?

NO .... 0 --->   GO TO Q.13, PAGE 7   45/

(OR)

YES, FROM:

(Circle All That Apply)

BELIZE	01	46/
COSTA RICA	02	47/
EL SALVADOR	03	48/
GUATEMALA	04	GO TO Q.3, NEXT PAGE 49/
HONDURAS	05	50/
NICARAGUA	06	51/
PANAMA	07	52/
THE PHILIPPINES	08	53/

SHOW
CARD
A

CARD 01

3. Para establecer a quien he de entrevistar en su hogar, necesito hacerle unas cuantas preguntas más acerca de usted y de las personas que viven en (esta casa/este apartamento). Primero, vamos a empezar con usted. ¿Me podría decir su nombre, su edad, y el lugar donde nació?

Ahora, quisiera hacer una lista de todos los demás adultos y niños que viven aquí. Me podría decir el nombre, la edad, y el lugar donde nació cada persona que vive aquí?   FILL IN HH ROSTER STARTING WITH INFORMANT.

- DO NOT INCLUDE PEOPLE WHO ARE AWAY ON ACTIVE MILITARY DUTY, LIVING AT SCHOOL, OR PEOPLE IN JAIL OR OTHER INSTITUTIONS.
- DO INCLUDE PEOPLE AWAY TEMPORARILY--ON VACATION, IN THE HOSPITAL FOR A FIXED STAY, ETC.
- BE SURE TO PROBE FOR ALL HOUSEHOLD MEMBERS.

3. FIRST NAME ONLY	4. SEX IF NECESSARY, ASK: ¿Es (NAME) hombre o mujer?	5. AGE ON LAST BIRTHDAY	6. COUNTRY OF ORIGIN
			Country Codes List Belize ...... 01 Nicaragua ..... 06 Costa Rica ....02 Panama .... 07 El Salvador .... 03 The Philippines. 08 Guatemala ... 04 U.S. .... 09 Honduras ..... 05 Other 10
INFORMANT: 01. _____ 54/	Hombre .... 1 Mujer 2 55/	AGE: ☐☐ 56-57/	COUNTRY CODE: ☐☐ 58-59/ If other, what? _____ 60-61/
OTHER HH MEMBERS: 02. _____ 62/	Hombre .... 1 Mujer 2 63/	AGE: ☐☐ 64-65/	COUNTRY CODE: ☐☐ 66-67/ If other, what? _____ 68-69/
(REPEAT 4-6 FOR EACH HH MEMBER) 03. _____ 70/	Hombre .... 1 Mujer 2 71/	AGE: ☐☐ 72-73/	COUNTRY CODE: ☐☐ 74-75/ If other, what? _____ 76-77/
04. _____ 9/	Hombre .... 1 Mujer 2 10/	AGE: ☐☐ 11-12/	COUNTRY CODE: ☐☐ 13-14/ (CARD 02) 7-8/ 1-6/ If other, what? _____ 15-16/
05. _____ 17/	Hombre .... 1 Mujer 2 18/	AGE: ☐☐ 19-20/	COUNTRY CODE: ☐☐ 21-22/ If other, what? _____ 23-24/
06. _____ 25/	Hombre .... 1 Mujer 2 26/	AGE: ☐☐ 27-28/	COUNTRY CODE: ☐☐ 29-30/ If other, what? _____ 31-32/
07. _____ 33/	Hombre .... 1 Mujer 2 34/	AGE: ☐☐ 35-36/	COUNTRY CODE: ☐☐ 37-38/ If other, what? _____ 39-40/
08. _____ 41/	Hombre .... 1 Mujer 2 42/	AGE: ☐☐ 43-44/	COUNTRY CODE: ☐☐ 45-46/ If other, what? _____ 47-48/
09. _____ 49/	Hombre .... 1 Mujer 2 50/	AGE: ☐☐ 51-52/	COUNTRY CODE: ☐☐ 53-54/ If other, what? _____ 55-56/
10. _____ 57/	Hombre .... 1 Mujer 2 58/	AGE: ☐☐ 59-60/	COUNTRY CODE: ☐☐ 61-62/ If other, what? _____ 63-64/

CARD 01 / 02

4

7. Para estar absolutamente seguro de que no he pasado por alto a nadie, ¿hay acaso alguna persona más que vive aquí, por lo general, que usted no me haya mencionado -- incluyendo a las criaturas y a los niños pequeños?

(Circle One)

YES .... 1 --> ENTER NAME IN ROSTER, ASK Q.3-Q.6

NO .... 2 --> CONTINUE WITH Q.8

65/

8. INTERVIEWER CHECK ROSTER TO DETERMINE IF HOUSEHOLD IS ELIGIBLE FOR MAIN INTERVIEW:

HOW MANY HOUSEHOLD MEMBERS ARE AGE 18-64 (AND) BORN IN EITHER EL SALVADOR (OR) THE PHILIPPINES?

(Circle One)

NONE .... 0 --> CONTINUE WITH Q.9

ONE .... 1 --> GO TO Q.10, NEXT PAGE

TWO OR MORE 2

66/

9. IF NO HH MEMBER BORN IN EL SALVADOR/PHILIPPINES, FOLLOW INSTRUCTIONS BELOW:

9A. INTERVIEWER CHECK ROSTER:

WERE ANY HH MEMBERS AGE 18-64 BORN IN THE FOLLOWING SIX CENTRAL AMERICAN COUNTRIES? ——>

ELIGIBLE COUNTRIES:

Belize
Costa Rica
Guatemala
Honduras
Nicaragua
Panama

(Circle One)

YES .... 1 ---> ANSWER Q.9B

NO .... 2 ---> GO TO Q.13, PAGE 7

67/

9B. IF YES TO Q.9A, SAY: Estamos interesados en hablar con gente de otros países que los E.E.U.U. Es posible que le pidamos a usted, o a alguna otra persona en su hogar, que participe en otra entrevista acerca de lo que le ha pasado desde que vino a Los Angeles. Esta entrevista será más o menos dentro de un mes. Quisiera saber, en caso de que lo seleccionemos a usted, o que seleccionemos a alguna otra persona en su hogar para que participe en la segunda parte de esta investigación, ¿cuál es el mejor momento para comunicarme con usted para que le pueda explicar esta encuesta y para que averigüe si las personas que viven en su hogar quieren participar en esta investigación? RECORD BEST TIME TO CALL BACK ON CASE RECORD FOLDER.

* ASK INFORMANT FOR HIS/HER FIRST AND LAST NAME SO WE CAN RECONTACT HIM/HER *

( ) CHECK HERE AND FILL OUT RECONTACT FORM ON PAGE 6.

CARD 02

5

THIS PAGE FOR HH MEMBERS BORN IN EL SALVADOR OR THE PHILIPPINES:

10. **ONE ELIGIBLE HOUSEHOLD MEMBER BORN IN EL SALVADOR OR THE PHILIPPINES, SAY:**

Estamos interesados en hablar con gente que nació en otros países. Quisiera invitar a (ELIGIBLE RESPONDENT) a participar en una segunda entrevista--más o menos dentro de un mes--para responder a más preguntas sobre sus experiencias viviendo y trabajando en Los Angeles. ¿Me podría decir el nombre y apellido de (ELIGIBLE RESPONDENT)? ¿Esta aquí en este momento? ¿Quisiera saber cuál es el mejor momento para comunicarme con (usted/él/ella) para hacer una cita para explicarle esta encuesta y averigüar si (usted/él/ella) podrá participar en otra entrevista, (más o menos dentro de un mes)?   RECORD BEST TIME TO CALL BACK ON CASE RECORD FOLDER.

RECORD NAME OF ELIGIBLE R ON CASE RECORD FOLDER AND ENTER   Line No. on Roster: ▢▢   68-69/
PERSON'S LINE NUMBER FROM THE ROSTER IN THESE BOXES:

( ) CHECK HERE AND FILL OUT RECONTACT FORM ON PAGE 6.

11. **MORE THAN ONE ELIGIBLE HOUSEHOLD MEMBER BORN IN EL SALVADOR OR THE PHILIPPINES, SAY:**

11A.   Estamos interesados en hablar con gente que nació en otros países. Para asegurarme que hablo con quien corresponde, ¿me puede decir cuál de estas personas (READ NAMES OF ELIGIBLE HH MEMBERS) ha cumplido años más recientemente?

RECORD NAME OF ELIGIBLE R ON CASE RECORD FOLDER AND ENTER   Line No. on Roster: ▢▢   70-71/
PERSON'S LINE NUMBER FROM THE ROSTER IN THESE BOXES:

11B.   Quisiera invitar a (ELIGIBLE RESPONDENT) a participar en una segunda entrevista--más o menos dentro de un mes--para responder a más preguntas sobre sus experiencias viviendo y trabajando en Los Angeles. ¿Me podría decir el nombre y apellido de (ELIGIBLE RESPONDENT)? ¿Esta aquí en este momento? ¿Quisiera saber cuál es el mejor momento para comunicarme con (usted/él/ella) para hacer una cita para explicarle esta encuesta y averigüar si (usted/él/ella) podrá participar en otra entrevista, (más o menos dentro de un mes)?   RECORD BEST TIME TO CALL BACK ON CASE RECORD FOLDER.

( ) CHECK HERE AND FILL OUT RECONTACT FORM ON PAGE 6.

CARD 02

6

RECONTACT FORM FOR ELIGIBLE HOUSEHOLDS ONLY
(El Salvador/Philippines/Other Eligible Central American Country)

12. En caso de que se haya mudado o si no podemos localizarlo/localizarla cuando volvamos para hacer la entrevista (aproximadamente dentro de un mes), ¿me puede proporcionar los nombres, las direcciones, y los números de teléfono de tres personas que sabrán como encontrarlo/encontrarla? Podrían ser, por ejemplo, sus padres, sus abuelos, una tía o un tío, otro pariente, o un amigo -- cualquier persona con quien usted esté seguro de que guardará contacto. (ASK R TO LOOK UP ADDRESS, PHONE NUMBER.)

INTERVIEWER CHECK:		72/
ENTER NUMBER OF CONTACTS GIVEN:	NONE - REFUSED INFORMATION	0
	ONE NAME	1
	TWO NAMES	2
	THREE NAMES	3

A. _____
   Apellido   Nombre

   _____
   Calle y número

   _____
   Ciudad   Estado   Zona postal

   ( )
   _____
   Código telefónico   Teléfono

   ¿Cuál es el parentezco o relación que usted tiene con esta persona?
   (Por ejemplo, su madre, padre, abuela, tía, hermana, amigo, etc.)

   _____
   Parentezco o relación que usted tiene con esta persona

B. _____
   Apellido   Nombre

   _____
   Calle y número

   _____
   Ciudad   Estado   Zona postal

   ( )
   _____
   Código telefónico   Teléfono

   ¿Cuál es el parentezco o relación que usted tiene con esta persona?
   (Por ejemplo, su madre, padre, abuela, tía, hermana, amigo, etc.)

   _____
   Parentezco o relación que usted tiene con esta persona

C. _____
   Apellido   Nombre

   _____
   Calle y número

   _____
   Ciudad   Estado   Zona postal

   ( )
   _____
   Código telefónico   Teléfono

   ¿Cuál es el parentezco o relación que usted tiene con esta persona?
   (Por ejemplo, su madre, padre, abuela, tía, hermana, amigo, etc.)

   _____
   Parentezco o relación que usted tiene con esta persona

```
THANK R AND REMIND HIM/HER THAT A RAND INTERVIEWER
(WILL/MAY) RECONTACT HIM/HER IN ABOUT ONE MONTH.
LEAVE COPY OF QUESTION AND ANSWER SHEET.

                    (GO TO Q.13 NEXT PAGE)
```

CARD 02

7

FOR EVERYONE:

13. Aquí concluye esta entrevista. Sólo necesito hacerle un par de preguntas más para incluir esta información en nuestro archivo.

A. ¿Hay un teléfono en esta residencia para poder comunicarse con usted?

(Circle One)

YES 1

NO 2   9/

14. En caso que mi oficina quiera asegurarse que estuve aquí para llevar a cabo esta entrevista, cuál es su número de teléfono?

Código telefónico	Teléfono

OR

REFUSED .... R   10/

Mucha gracias por haber participado en esta importante encuesta. Le agradecemos mucho su ayuda.

IF ELIGIBLE HOUSEHOLD: REMEMBER TO LEAVE A COPY OF THE RAND QUESTION AND ANSWER SHEET AND REMIND R THAT AN INTERVIEWER WILL RECONTACT HIM/HER IN ABOUT ONE MONTH.

INTERVIEWER RECORD TIME ENDED:

☐☐ : ☐☐   11-14/

AM 1

PM 2   15/

CARD 03

1

INTRODUCTION TO SCREENER INTERVIEW

Kamusta, ang pangalan ko ay si _____. Ako ay taga RAND, isang organisasyong taga pagsaliksik sa Santa Monica. (Ipakita ang identipikasyon at sulat ng introduksiyon). Magtanong kung maari makipag-usap sa isang matandang miyembro ng tahanan. (SHOW RAND IDENTIFICATION CARD AND INTRODUCTORY LETTER). ASK TO SPEAK TO AN ADULT HOUSEHOLD MEMBER.

Anong salita ang gusto mong gamitin natin:

Ingles o Tagalog?

Kami ay nagsasagawa ng pagsusuri tungkol sa mga pamilyang taga ibang bansa upang malaman kung paano sila nakakaangkop sa pamumuhay dito sa Los Angeles. Ang pagtatanong na ito ay tatagal lamang ng limang minuto, at ang pagtatanong na ito ay lubos na kusang loob. Nais naming tulungan ninyo kami, ngayong araw na ito sa pamamagitan ng pagsagot ninyo sa mga tanong tungkol sa mga taong nakatira sa kabahayang ito, katulad ng, kung anong salita ang laging ginagamit sa tahanan na ito, kung ilang taong gulang at kung saan ipinanganak ang mga miyembro ng inyong tahanan.

Nais kong mag-umpisa ng pagtatanong ngayon kung OK sa inyo--tatagal lamang ito ng limang minuto.

A.   Una, ano ba ang salita na laging ginagamit sa inyong bahay. RECORD INFORMATION IN ITEM F ON COVER OF SCREENER.

Magsimula ng "Screener" na pagtatanong.

LANGUAGE HH USUALLY SPEAKS

- IF R HAS QUESTIONS, USE SUGGESTED ANSWERS ON THE "QUESTION AND ANSWER SHEET."
- IF ADULT IS NOT AVAILABLE, SCHEDULE AN APPOINTMENT AND RECORD ON CASE RECORD FOLDER.
- IF R REFUSES OR BREAKS OFF THE INTERVIEW, COMPLETE THE REFUSAL/BREAKOFF FORM.

2

37–40/

41/

42–43/

44/

45/

INTERVIEWER RECORD TIME STARTED:

AM 1
PM 2

1. Una, mayroon akong mga tanong tungkol sa mga taong nakatira dito (bahay/apartment). Isipin ninyo ang lahat ng taong nakatira dito - mga matanda, bata at sanggol. Huwag ninyong ibilang ang mga nasa aktibong serbisyo militar o kaya'y nakatira sa iskwela o kolehiyo, o kaya iyong natutulog sa ibang lugar kadalasan.

Kasama ang sarili ninyo, ilan ang mga taong nakatira dito?

NUMBER OF
HOUSEHOLD MEMBERS:

2. Kayo ba, o sino man sa mga taong nakatira dito (bahay/apartment) ay ipinanganak sa labas ng Estados Unidos?

(Circle One)

YES .... 1 ---> ANSWER A

NO—ALL HOUSEHOLD MEMBERS
WERE BORN IN THE U.S. .... 2 ---> GO TO Q.13, PAGE 7

A. HAND CARD TO R. Kayo ba, o sino man sa mga taong nakatira dito (bahay/apartment) ay ipinanganak sa alin mang bansa na nakalista sa tarheta na ito?
IF YES, ASK: Alin dito?

SHOW
CARD
A

NO .... 0 ---> GO TO Q.13, PAGE 7

(OR)

YES, FROM: (Circle All That Apply)

BELIZE 01
COSTA RICA 02
EL SALVADOR 03
GUATEMALA 04   GO TO Q.3, NEXT PAGE
HONDURAS 05
NICARAGUA 06
PANAMA 07
THE PHILIPPINES 08

46/
47/
48/
49/
50/
51/
52/
53/

CARD 01

3

3. Kami ay higit na interesado na makausap ang mga tao na galing sa (COUNTRIES LISTED IN Q.2A). para malaman namin kung sino ang dapat na tanungin dito sa inyong kabahay. Kailangang makapagtanong pa ako ng ilang katanungan tungkol sa i yo at sa mga taong nakatira dito (bahay/apartment). Una, magsimula tayo sa iyo, maari bang ibigay mo sa akin ang iyong (una at huli) pangalan?

Susunod, nais kong ilista ang lahat ng pangalan ng iba pang matatanda at mga bata na nakatira dito.   FILL IN HH ROSTER STARTING WITH INFORMANT.

- DO NOT INCLUDE PEOPLE WHO ARE AWAY ON ACTIVE MILITARY DUTY, LIVING AT SCHOOL, OR PEOPLE IN JAIL OR OTHER INSTITUTIONS.
- DO INCLUDE PEOPLE AWAY TEMPORARILY—ON VACATION, IN THE HOSPITAL FOR A FIXED STAY, ETC.
- BE SURE TO PROBE FOR ALL HOUSEHOLD MEMBERS.

3. FIRST NAME ONLY	4. SEX IF NECESSARY, ASK: SI (NAME) ba ay lalaki o babae?	5. AGE ON LAST BIRTHDAY	6. COUNTRY OF ORIGIN
			Country Codes List Belize .... 01 Nicaragua ...... 06 Costa Rica.... 02 Panama .... 07 El Salvador ... 03 The Philippines . 08 Guatemala .... 04 U.S. .... 09 Honduras...... 05 Other.......... 10
INFORMANT: 01. _____ 54/	Lalaki.........1 Babae 2 55/	AGE: 56-57/	COUNTRY CODE: 58-59/ If other, what? 60-61/
OTHER HH MEMBERS: (REPEAT 4-6 FOR EACH HH MEMBER) 02. _____ 62/	Lalaki.........1 Babae 2 63/	AGE: 64-65/	COUNTRY CODE: 66-67/ If other, what? 68-69/
03. _____ 70/	Lalaki.........1 Babae 2 71/	AGE: 72-73/	COUNTRY CODE: 74-75/ If other, what? 76-77/
			CARD 02 7-8/
04. _____ 9/	Lalaki.........1 Babae 2 10/	AGE: 11-12/	COUNTRY CODE: 13-14/ If other, what? 15-16/
05. _____ 17/	Lalaki.........1 Babae 2 18/	AGE: 19-20/	COUNTRY CODE: 21-22/ If other, what? 23-24/
06. _____ 25/	Lalaki.........1 Babae 2 26/	AGE: 27-28/	COUNTRY CODE: 29-30/ If other, what? 31-32/
07. _____ 33/	Lalaki.........1 Babae 2 34/	AGE: 35-36/	COUNTRY CODE: 37-38/ If other, what? 39-40/
08. _____ 41/	Lalaki.........1 Babae 2 42/	AGE: 43-44/	COUNTRY CODE: 45-46/ If other, what? 47-48/
09. _____ 49/	Lalaki.........1 Babae 2 50/	AGE: 51-52/	COUNTRY CODE: 53-54/ If other, what? 55-56/
10. _____ 57/	Lalaki.........1 Babae 2 58/	AGE: 59-60/	COUNTRY CODE: 61-62/ If other, what? 63-64/

CARD 01 / 02

4

7. Upang makatiyak, mayroon pa bang ibang tao na laging tumitira dito na hindi mo nasabi sa akin - pati na mga sanggol at maliliit na mga bata?

(Circle One)

YES .... 1 —> ENTER NAME IN ROSTER, ASK Q.3-Q.6

NO .... 2 —> CONTINUE WITH Q.8

65/

8. INTERVIEWER CHECK ROSTER TO DETERMINE IF HOUSEHOLD IS ELIGIBLE FOR MAIN INTERVIEW:

HOW MANY HOUSEHOLD MEMBERS ARE AGE 18-64 (AND) BORN IN EITHER EL SALVADOR (OR) THE PHILIPPINES?

(Circle One)

NONE .... 0 —> CONTINUE WITH Q.9
ONE .... 1 —> GO TO Q.10, NEXT PAGE
TWO OR MORE .... 2 —> GO TO Q.11, NEXT PAGE

66/

9. IF NO HH MEMBER BORN IN EL SALVADOR/PHILIPPINES, FOLLOW INSTRUCTIONS BELOW:

9A.   INTERVIEWER CHECK ROSTER:

WERE ANY HH MEMBERS AGE 18-64 BORN IN THE FOLLOWING SIX CENTRAL AMERICAN COUNTRIES?

ELGIBLE COUNTRIES:

Belize
Costa Rica
Guatemala
Honduras
Nicaragua
Panama

(Circle One)

YES .... 1 —> ANSWER Q.9B

NO .... 2 —> GO TO Q.13, PAGE 7

67/

9B.   IF YES TO Q.9A, SAY: Ikaw o kahit na sino na nakatira dito sa inyong kabahay ay maaaring makasali sa susunod na pagtatanong tungkol sa iyong mga karanasan sa pagtira sa Los Angeles. Ang pagtatanong na iyon ay gagawin sa isang buwan. Kung sakaling ikaw o sino pa man dito sa inyo ay napili na sumali sa ikalwang bahagi ng pagaaral, gusto kong malaman ang pinakamabuting oras na matawagan kayo upang aking maitakda ang ating pagtatagpo upang maipaliwanag ko ang tungkol sa pagaaral at nang malaman ko kung ang iyong kabahay ay nais sumali. RECORD BEST TIME TO CALL BACK ON CASE RECORD FOLDER.

* ASK INFORMANT FOR HIS/HER FIRST AND LAST NAME SO WE CAN RECONTACT HIM/HER *

( ) CHECK HERE AND FILL OUT RECONTACT FORM ON PAGE 6.

CARD 02

5

THIS PAGE FOR HH MEMBERS BORN IN EL SALVADOR OR THE PHILIPPINES:

10. **ONE ELIGIBLE HOUSEHOLD MEMBER BORN IN EL SALVADOR OR THE PHILIPPINES, SAY:**

(Mayroon akong katanungan na itatanong (ELIGIBLE RESPONDENT), si (pangalan) ay naririto ba ngayon?) Gusto kong malaman kung ano ang pinakamabuting oras na matawagan (ikaw/sila) upang maitakda ko ang pagtatagpo para maipaliwanag ang tungkol sa pagaaral at nang malaman ko tuloy kung (ikaw/sila) ay maaring sumali sa mga isang buwan. RECORD BEST TIME TO CALL BACK ON CASE RECORD FOLDER.

68–69/

RECORD NAME OF ELIGIBLE R ON CASE RECORD FOLDER AND ENTER
PERSON'S LINE NUMBER FROM THE ROSTER IN THESE BOXES: ➔ Line No. on Roster: ☐☐

( ) CHECK HERE AND FILL OUT RECONTACT FORM ON PAGE 6.

11. **MORE THAN ONE ELIGIBLE HOUSEHOLD MEMBER BORN IN EL SALVADOR OR THE PHILIPPINES, SAY:**

11A. Upang makatiyak na ako ay makikipagusap sa tamang tao, masasabi mo ba sa akin kung sino sa mga taong ito (READ NAMES OF ELIGIBLE HH MEMBERS), ang may pinakamalapit na nakaraang kaarawan?

70–71/

RECORD NAME OF ELIGIBLE R ON CASE RECORD FOLDER AND ENTER
PERSON'S LINE NUMBER FROM THE ROSTER IN THESE BOXES: ➔ Line No. on Roster: ☐☐

11B. (Mayroon akong mga katanungan na itatanong (ELIGIBLE RESPONDENT) si (pangalan) ba ay naririto ngayon?) Gusto kong malaman ang pinakamabuting oras na matawagan (ikaw/sila) upang maitakda ko ang pagtatagpo para maipaliwanag ang tungkol sa pagaaral at nang malaman ko tuloy kung (ikaw/sila) ay maaring sumali sa pagtatanong na gagawin sa mga isang buwan. RECORD BEST TIME TO CALL BACK ON CASE RECORD FOLDER.

( ) CHECK HERE AND FILL OUT RECONTACT FORM ON PAGE 6.

CARD 02

RECONTACT FORM FOR ELIGIBLE HOUSEHOLDS ONLY

(El Salvador/Philippines/Other Eligible Central American Country)

72/

12. Kung sakaling kayo ay makalipat ng tirahan at hindi namin kayo matagpuan sa pagtatanong (sa mga isang buwan), maaari po bang makuha ang mga pangalan, tirahan at numero ng telepono ng tatlong tao na maaring makaalam kung paano kayo matatagpuan. Halimbawa, maaring ito'y iyong mga magulang, lolo/lola, tiya o tiyo, mga ibang kamaganak, o kaibigan - kahit sinong tao na tiyak na makikipagugnayan ka. (ASK R TO LOOK UP ADDRESS, PHONE NUMBER.)

INTERVIEWER CHECK:	
ENTER NUMBER OF CONTACTS GIVEN:	NONE - REFUSED INFORMATION 0
	ONE NAME 1
	TWO NAMES 2
	THREE NAMES 3

A.

Huling Pangalan _____ Una _____

Numero at Kalye ng tirahan _____

Syudad _____ State _____ Zip _____

( ) _____
Area Code   Telepono

Ano ang relasyon ng taong ito sa iyo? (Halimbawa, ina, ama, lola, tiya, kapatid na babae, kaibigan, at iba pa)

_____
Relasyon ng tao sa iyo

B.

Huling Pangalan _____ Una _____

Numero at Kalye ng tirahan _____

Syudad _____ State _____ Zip _____

( ) _____
Area Code   Telepono

Ano ang relasyon ng taong ito sa iyo? (Halimbawa, ina, ama, lola, tiya, kapatid na babae, kaibigan, at iba pa)

_____
Relasyon ng tao sa iyo

C.

Huling Pangalan _____ Una _____

Numero at Kalye ng tirahan _____

Syudad _____ State _____ Zip _____

( ) _____
Area Code   Telepono

Ano ang relasyon ng taong ito sa iyo? (Halimbawa, ina, ama, lola, tiya, kapatid na babae, kaibigan, at iba pa)

_____
Relasyon ng tao sa iyo

THANK R AND REMIND HIM/HER THAT A RAND INTERVIEWER (WILL/MAY) RECONTACT HIM/HER IN ABOUT ONE MONTH. LEAVE COPY OF QUESTION AND ANSWER SHEET.

(GO TO Q.13 NEXT PAGE)

CARD 02

7

CARD 03   7-8/
                                                                             1-6/

FOR EVERYONE:

13. Iyan ang katapusan ng pagtatanong na ito. Kailangan ko lamang magtanong ng
    dalawang huling katanungan para sa aming pagiingat ng ulat.

    A. Mayroon bang telepono ang bahay na ito na maari kayong tawagan?

                                                    (Circle One)   9/

                        YES 1

                        NO 2

14. Kung sakaling ang opisina ko ay nais makatiyak na ako ay naririto ngayon para sa pagtatanong, ano
    ang numero ng telepono ninyo?

        ⎧
        ⎨ _____   _____
        ⎩ Area Code   Telephone

                  OR

                        REFUSED .... R   10/

Salamat sa pagsali ninyo sa mahalagang pag-aaral na ito. Ikinalulugod
namin ang inyong tulong.

**IF ELIGIBLE HOUSEHOLD: REMEMBER TO LEAVE A COPY OF THE RAND QUESTION AND ANSWER SHEET AND REMIND
R THAT AN INTERVIEWER WILL RECONTACT HIM/HER IN ABOUT ONE MONTH.**

INTERVIEWER RECORD TIME ENDED: ☐☐ : ☐☐   11-14/

                                   AM 1   15/

                                   PM 2

                                                                              CARD 03

MAIN INTERVIEW QUESTIONNAIRE

Revision 7/15/91

LOS ANGELES COMMUNITY SURVEY
MAIN INTERVIEW

CARD 01   7-8/

BARCODE ID LABEL   1-6/

FORM TYPE: |M|I| 9-10/

C. TOTAL NUMBER OF CALLS: |__|__| 14-15/

D. DATE CASE FINALIZED: |__|__| / |__|__| / |9|1| 16-21/
                          MONTH   DAY   YEAR

E. LENGTH OF INTERVIEW: |__|__|__| 22-24/
                          (MINUTES)

F. INTERVIEWER'S NAME & ID:

    _____ |__|__|__|__| 25-28/
    (NAME)   (ID #)

A. FINAL STATUS: 11-12/

    COMPLETE 01
    BREAKOFF 02
    REFUSAL 03
    LANGUAGE BARRIER 04
        (Which? _____)
    ILLNESS/SENILITY 05
    INACCESSIBLE 06
    VACANCY 07
    ELIGIBLE R MOVED 08
    MAXIMUM CALLS 09
    FIELD PERIOD ENDED 10
    OTHER (SPECIFY) 11

B. INTERVIEW CONDUCTED IN: 13/

    ENGLISH 1
    SPANISH 2
    TAGALOG 3
    OTHER 4
        (What? _____)
    NO INTERVIEW 5

Prepared by:

RAND
1700 Main Street
Santa Monica, CA   90407-2138

INTRODUCTION

A. Hello, my name is _____ and I'm from RAND, a research organization in Santa Monica. SHOW RAND IDENTIFICATION CARD AND LETTER OF INTRODUCTION. Can I speak with (NAME OF ELIGIBLE RESPONDENT)?

B. How would you prefer that I speak with you:

    In English, or

    SPANISH: O si usied prefiere, en Español?

    TAGALOG: Kung gusto mo ay sa Tagalog.

C. Several weeks ago, I spoke with _____ about a survey we're conducting. We're trying to find out how people from (the Philippines/El Salvador/Central American countries) adjust to living in Los Angeles.

    We'd like you to help us today by answering some questions about living and working in the U.S. The interview takes about 30 to 45 minutes and we think you'll find it interesting. If you participate, we'll give you a $5.00 gift certificate to use at your local grocery store to thank you for your time.

D. Before we begin:
    I'd like to go over some important things about this study. First, I want to assure you that this interview is voluntary. You can refuse to participate or refuse to answer any questions. Also your answers will be kept absolutely private.

E. Do you have any questions?
    I'd like to begin now if it is OK with you.

RECORD TIME STARTED: ☐☐ : ☐☐

AM 1
PM 2

29-32/
33/

SECTION A: RESPONDENT BACKGROUND

The first group of questions are about you and your background.

A1.   INTERVIEWER, CODE WITHOUT ASKING:

(Circle One)

R IS MALE 1
R IS FEMALE 2

34/

A2.   How old were you on your last birthday?

AGE: ☐☐   35-36/

A3.   In what country were you born?

(Circle One)

BELIZE 1   37/
COSTA RICA 2
EL SALVADOR 3
GUATEMALA 4
HONDURAS 5   } GO TO A4
NICARAGUA 6
PANAMA 7
THE PHILIPPINES 8
U.S. OR OTHER COUNTRY (SPECIFY) 9   --> ASK A3a

_____

A3a.   That's the end of this interview. For the purposes of this study. We're only interviewing people who were born in the Philippines, El Salvador, or other Central American countries. THANK RESPONDENT AND END INTERVIEW.

CARD 01

1

A4. What is the highest grade or year of school or college you completed in (COUNTRY OF ORIGIN)?

(Circle One)   38-39/

NO FORMAL SCHOOLING 99
KINDERGARTEN 00
1ST GRADE 01
2ND GRADE 02
3RD GRADE 03
4TH GRADE 04
5TH GRADE 05
6TH GRADE 06
7TH GRADE 07
8TH GRADE 08
9TH GRADE 09
10TH GRADE 10
11TH GRADE 11
12TH GRADE 12
1 YEAR OF COLLEGE 13
2 YEARS OF COLLEGE 14
3 YEARS OF COLLEGE 15
4 YEARS OF COLLEGE 16
5 YEARS OF COLLEGE OR MORE 17

A5. Did you *ever* attend regular school or college in the U.S.?

(Circle One)

YES .... 1 --> ASK A6   40/
NO .... 2 --> GO TO A7

A6. What is the highest grade or year of school or college you completed in the U.S.?

(Circle One)   41-42/

ATTENDED SOME SCHOOLING IN U.S. BUT DIDN'T COMPLETE A GRADE OR YEAR 99
KINDERGARTEN 00
1ST GRADE 01
2ND GRADE 02
3RD GRADE 03
4TH GRADE 04
5TH GRADE 05
6TH GRADE 06
7TH GRADE 07
8TH GRADE 08
9TH GRADE 09
10TH GRADE 10
11TH GRADE 11
12TH GRADE (OR GED) 12
1 YEAR OF COLLEGE 13
2 YEARS OF COLLEGE 14
3 YEARS OF COLLEGE 15
4 YEARS OF COLLEGE 16
5 YEARS OF COLLEGE OR MORE 17

CARD 01

2

A7.   The next question is about the language you usually speak with your relatives and friends.

Do you speak to (READ PERSON) in only English, mostly English, mostly (Spanish/Tagalog), or only (Spanish/Tagalog)?

(Circle One Number on Each Line)

	ONLY ENGLISH	MOSTLY ENGLISH	BOTH EQUALLY	MOSTLY SPANISH/ TAGALOG	ONLY SPANISH/ TAGALOG	NOT APPLICABLE	
a. Your (husband/wife)?	1	2	3	4	5	9	43/
b. Your parents or older relatives?	1	2	3	4	5	9	44/
c. Your brothers and sisters?	1	2	3	4	5	9	45/
d. Your children?	1	2	3	4	5	9	46/
e. Your co-workers?	1	2	3	4	5	9	47/
f. Your supervisor?	1	2	3	4	5	9	48/
g. Your friends and neighbors?	1	2	3	4	5	9	49/

A8.   How well do you (READ STATEMENTS BELOW)--would you say very well, well, some, a little, or not at all?

(Circle One Number on Each Line)

	VERY WELL	WELL	SOME	A LITTLE	NOT AT ALL	
a. Read newspapers and books in English	1	2	3	4	5	50/
b. Write letters in English	1	2	3	4	5	51/
c. Understand a conversation in English	1	2	3	4	5	52/
d. Carry on a conversation in English	1	2	3	4	5	53/
e. Read newspapers and books in (Spanish/Tagalog)	1	2	3	4	5	54/
f. Write letters in (Spanish/Tagalog)	1	2	3	4	5	55/

CARD 01

3

A9. Next I'm going to read you a list of activities. Please tell me how often you actually do each of these things. How often do you (READ ITEM)--
Would you say... <u>everyday, a few times a week, a few times a month, a few times a year, or never?</u>

(Circle One Number on Each Line)

	EVERY DAY	A FEW TIMES A WEEK	A FEW TIMES A MONTH	A FEW TIMES A YEAR	NEVER	NOT APPLICABLE OR NOT AVAILABLE	
a. Watch (Spanish/Tagalog) language TV programs?	1	2	3	4	5	9	56/
b. Listen to (Spanish/Tagalog) language radio programs?	1	2	3	4	5	9	57/
c. Read (Spanish/Tagalog) language newspapers or magazines?	1	2	3	4	5	9	58/
d. Watch English language TV programs?	1	2	3	4	5	9	59/
e. Listen to English language radio programs?	1	2	3	4	5	9	60/
f. Read English language newspapers or magazines?	1	2	3	4	5	9	61/

4

CARD 01

A10. Have you *ever* attended classes to learn English since you came to the U.S.?

(Circle One)

YES..........1 --> ASK A11   9/
NO...........2 --> GO TO A15

A11. Are you *currently* attending classes to learn English?

(Circle One)

YES..........1   10/
NO...........2

A12. How long (have you been attending/did you attend) classes to learn English? PROBE FOR NUMBER OF DAYS/WEEKS/MONTHS.

COURSE LENGTH: _____   11-12/

CODE UNIT: (Circle One)   13/

DAYS..........1
WEEKS.........2
MONTHS........3
YEARS.........4
OTHER (SPECIFY)....5

A13. How many hours of classes to learn English (do/did) you attend each week?

HOURS PER WEEK: [   ]   14-15/

CARD 02
7-8/
1-6/

A14. (Are you attending/Did you attend) classes to learn English because of amnesty requirements?

(Circle One)

YES..........1 --> GO TO A16
NO...........2 --> GO TO A16   16/

A15. Why didn't you attend classes to learn English? PROBE: Anything else?

_____
_____

(Circle All That Apply)

NONE AVAILABLE..........01   17-18/
CLASSES COST TOO MUCH..........02   19-20/
CLASSES WERE ALWAYS AT A BAD TIME..........03   21-22/
CLASSES WERE FULL OR CLOSED..........04   23-24/
ALREADY KNEW ENOUGH ENGLISH..........05   25-26/
WORRIED THAT COULDN'T UNDERSTAND THE INSTRUCTOR..........06   27-28/
THOUGHT CLASSES WOULD BE TOO DIFFICULT..........07   29-30/
SOMEONE ELSE IN HOUSEHOLD WAS ATTENDING..........08   31-32/
NO CHILD DAY CARE AVAILABLE..........09   33-34/
NO TRANSPORTATION AVAILABLE..........10   35-36/
TOO BUSY WITH OTHER THINGS, NO FREE TIME..........11   37-38/
OTHER REASON (SPECIFY) _____ 12   39-40/

CARD 02

5

A16. Since you came to the U.S., have you attended a vocational training program--that is, have you attended a program to learn a trade or job skills? (For example, training to become a mechanic or nursing assistant.)

(Circle One)

YES......... 1 --> ASK A17

NO.......... 2 --> GO TO A21   41/

A17. Are you currently attending a vocational training program?

(Circle One)

YES......... 1

NO.......... 2   42/

A18. What type of vocational training program (is/was) this? RECORD VERBATIM. (What skill did you learn?)

_____   43-44/

A19. How long (have you been attending/did you attend a vocational training program? PROBE FOR NUMBER OF DAYS/WEEKS/MONTHS.

COURSE LENGTH: _____   45-46/

CODE UNIT: (Circle One)

DAYS............ 1

WEEKS........... 2

MONTHS.......... 3

YEARS........... 4

OTHER (SPECIFY) 5   47/

A20. How many hours of vocational training classes (do/did) you attend each week?   48-49/

HOURS PER WEEK: [ ][ ]   GO TO SECTION B, NEXT PAGE

A21. Why didn't you attend a vocational training program? PROBE: Anything else?

_____
_____
_____

(Circle All That Apply)

ALREADY HAD A TRADE/SKILL	01	50-51/
NONE AVAILABLE	02	52-53/
PROGRAMS COST TOO MUCH	03	54-55/
COURSES WERE ALWAYS AT A BAD TIME	04	56-57/
PROGRAMS WERE FULL OR CLOSED	05	58-59/
DIDN'T KNOW ENOUGH ENGLISH	06	60-61/
SOMEONE ELSE IN HOUSEHOLD WAS ATTENDING	07	62-63/
NO CHILD DAY CARE AVAILABLE	08	64-65/
NO TRANSPORTATION AVAILABLE	09	66-67/
TOO BUSY WITH OTHER THINGS, NO FREE TIME	10	68-69/
NOT PLANNING TO WORK	11	70-71/
OTHER REASON (SPECIFY) _____	12	72-73/

CARD 02

CARD 03   7-8/
           1-6/

SECTION B: FAMILY BACKGROUND

Now I'd like to ask a few questions about the people in your family who usually live in your (house/apartment).

B1.   Counting yourself, how many people in your family live in your (house/apartment)? Please include adults, babies, and children who usually stay with you as a member of your family. By family, we mean people living here who are related to you by blood, marriage, or adoption.

PERSON LIVES ALONE (GO TO B19, PAGE 13) 01

OR

ENTER # OF FAMILY MEMBERS: ☐☐   9-10/

B2.   Does this include (READ LIST):

(Circle One Number for Each Question)

a.   Any babies or children who are five years old or younger?

YES............. 1 --> How many? _____   11/
NO............. 2   12-13/

b.   Any children or teenagers age six through seventeen?

YES............. 1 --> How many? _____   14/
NO............. 2   15-16/

c.   Any people between the ages of 18 and 64 years old?

YES............. 1 --> How many? _____   17/
NO............. 2   18-19/

d.   Any people age 65 or older?

YES............. 1 --> How many? _____   20/
NO............. 2   21-22/

e.   Any people who usually work for pay at least 15 hours per week?

YES............. 1 --> How many? _____   23/
NO............. 2   24-25/

CARD 03

7

B3. How many of the people in this household age 18 or older were born in the United States?

NONE 00

OR

ENTER # ADULTS IN HOUSEHOLD BORN IN U.S.: ☐☐ 26-27/

B4. Are you: (READ CATEGORIES)

(Circle One)

Married or living as married .... 1 --> ASK B5
Divorced 2
Separated .... 3 } GO TO B7
Widowed, or 4
Have you never been married? 5

28/

B5. Does your (husband/wife) currently live with you in this (house/apartment)?

(Circle One)

YES .... 1 --> GO TO B7
NO .... 2 --> ASK B6

29/

B6. Where does your (husband/wife) currently live—is it somewhere else in the U.S., in your home country, or in another country?

(Circle One)

ELSEWHERE IN U.S. 1
HOME COUNTRY 2
OTHER COUNTRY 3

30/

B7. Do any of the following people usually live here in your (house/apartment)? (READ LIST)

	YES	NO	
A. Your mother?	1	2	31/
B. Your father?	1	2	32/
C. Your brothers or sisters?	1	2	33/
D. Your grandparents?	1	2	34/
E. Your child or children?	1	2	35/
F. Other relatives?	1	2	36/

B7a. Not counting your relatives, are there other people who usually live here, such as friends or people who are not related to you?

(Circle One)

YES .... 1 --> How many? _____ 37/ 38-39/
NO 2

CARD 03

8

CHILDREN'S EDUCATION

B8. INTERVIEWER CHECK B2b, PAGE 7:

DO ANY CHILDREN AGES 6 TO 17 LIVE IN THE HOUSEHOLD?

(Circle One)

YES................ 1 --> ASK B9

NO................. 2 --> GO TO B19, PAGE 13

40/

B9. You mentioned earlier that there are _____ children between the ages of 6 and 17 who are living here with you.

B9a. How many of these children are your own children?

NONE................ 00 --> GO TO B19, PAGE 13

OR

ENTER # OF RESPONDENT'S CHILDREN WHO LIVE IN HOUSEHOLD: [ ] --> ASK B10

41-42/

B10. The following questions are about your own children between the ages of 6 and 17 who are living here with you.

B10a. How many of your children are in school now or will be attending in the fall? (Remember we're talking about your own children age 6 to 17 who live here with you)

NONE................ 00 --> GO TO B14, PAGE 10

OR

ENTER # OF CHILDREN IN SCHOOL: [ ] --> ASK B11

43-44/

B11. What type of school do your children attend--is it a public school, a parochial or church school, or a private school? If your children attend different types of schools, please tell me how many attend each type. (Remember, we're talking about your own children age 6 to 17 who live here with you.)

NUMBER OF CHILDREN AGE 6 TO 17 IN:

a. PUBLIC SCHOOL: [ ] 45-46/

b. PAROCHIAL OR CHURCH SCHOOL: [ ] 47-48/

c. PRIVATE SCHOOL: [ ] 49-50/

d. TOTAL IN SCHOOL IS: (a+b+c=d) [ ] 51-52/

B12. How many of your children are in elementary school, junior high or middle school, high school, or college? (Remember, we're talking about your own children age 6 to 17 who live here with you.)

NUMBER OF CHILDREN AGE 6 TO 17 IN:

a. ELEMENTARY SCHOOL: [ ] 53-54/

b. JUNIOR HIGH OR MIDDLE SCHOOL: [ ] 55-56/

c. HIGH SCHOOL: [ ] 57-58/

d. COLLEGE [ ] 59-60/

e. TOTAL IN SCHOOL IS: (a+b+c+d=e) [ ] 61-62/

CARD 03

9

QUESTIONS ABOUT CHILDREN WHO ARE NOT IN SCHOOL

B13. You may have mentioned this earlier but I need to verify that I have the correct information about your children's education. Do you have any children age 6 to 17 who are not in school now (and will not attend school in the fall)? Remember, we're talking about your children who currently live here with you.

(Circle One)

63/

YES .... 1 ---> ASK B13a - B14

NO .... 2 ---> GO TO B15, PAGE 11

B13a. How many of your children age 6 to 17 are not in school now (and will not attend school in the fall)?

ENTER # OF CHILDREN NOT IN SCHOOL:

64-65/

B14. What is the main reason that your (oldest) child is not in school now (and will not attend school in the fall)?

66-67/

(Circle One)

CHILD HAS TO WORK 01

CHILD DOES NOT SPEAK ENGLISH 02

CHILD WAS NOT INTERESTED IN SCHOOL 03

CHILD WAS EXPELLED/SUSPENDED 04

SCHOOL IS TOO DANGEROUS 05

CHILD GRADUATED FROM HIGH SCHOOL 06

CHILD BECAME PREGNANT/HAD A CHILD 07

CHILD GOT MARRIED 08

CHILD NOT DOING WELL IN SCHOOL 09

OTHER (SPECIFY) 10

B14a. INTERVIEWER, CHECK B10a, PAGE 9:

HOW MANY CHILDREN AGE 6 TO 17 DOES THE RESPONDENT HAVE WHO ARE IN SCHOOL NOW OR WILL BE ATTENDING IN THE FALL?

(Circle One)

68/

NONE .... 0 ---> GO TO B19, PAGE 13

1 CHILD .... 1 } ASK B15

2 OR MORE CHILDREN ... 2

CARD 03

10

CARD 04

7-8/
1-6/

OPINIONS ABOUT CHILD'S SCHOOL

B15. Think about the school that your (oldest) child attends. What do you think are the most serious problems in your (oldest) child's school? PROBE: What else?

(Circle All That Apply)

NO PROBLEMS	00	9-10/
DON'T KNOW	99	11-12/
DRINKING/ALCOHOLISM	01	13-14/
USE OF DRUGS	02	15-16/
LACK OF DISCIPLINE	03	17-18/
LACK OF PROPER FINANCIAL SUPPORT	04	19-20/
OVERCROWDING	05	21-22/
POOR CURRICULUM/POOR STANDARDS	06	23-24/
STUDENT PROBLEMS UNDERSTANDING ENGLISH	07	25-26/
PARENTS' LACK OF INTEREST	08	27-28/
TEACHER'S LACK OF INTEREST	09	29-30/
STUDENT'S LACK OF INTEREST/TRUANCY	10	31-32/
MORAL STANDARDS/DRESS CODE	11	33-34/
DIFFICULTY IN GETTING GOOD TEACHERS	12	35-36/
LACK OF RESPECT FOR TEACHERS/OTHER STUDENTS	13	37-38/
NOT ENOUGH TRAINED TEACHERS	14	39-40/
FIGHTING	15	41-42/
GANGS	16	43-44/
LACK OF PARENTAL INVOLVEMENT IN SCHOOL ACTIVITIES	17	45-46/
OTHER (SPECIFY)	18	47-48/

B16. In your opinion, what do you think your (oldest) child's school should do to better serve immigrant children and families? RECORD VERBATIM. PROBE: What else?

_____ 49-50/

_____ 51-52/

_____ 53-54/

_____

_____

B17. INTERVIEWER CHECK B11, PAGE 9:

DO ANY OF RESPONDENT'S CHILDREN ATTEND PAROCHIAL OR CHURCH SCHOOL, OR A PRIVATE SCHOOL?

(Circle One)

YES............ 1 --> ASK B18

NO............ 2 --> GO TO B19   55/

CARD 04

11

CARD 05   7-8/
           1-6/

CARD 05

| | ASK IF R HAS CHILD IN PAROCHIAL OR PRIVATE SCHOOL |

B18. You and your family have decided to send your (child/children) to a parochial or private school. Could you tell me why you did not send your (child/children) to your local neighborhood public school? PROBE: Did you have any other reasons?

(Circle All That Apply)

QUALITY OF TEACHING STAFF	01	9-10/
STUDENT DISCIPLINE	02	11-12/
CURRICULUM/SUBJECTS TAUGHT	03	13-14/
SIZE OF CLASS	04	15-16/
SIZE OF SCHOOL	05	17-18/
GRADES/TEST SCORES OF STUDENT BODY	06	19-20/
TRACK RECORD OF GRADUATES	07	21-22/
PROXIMITY OF SCHOOL TO HOME	08	23-24/
EXTRACURRICULAR ACTIVITIES	09	25-26/
SOCIAL AND ECONOMIC BACKGROUND OF STUDENT BODY	10	27-28/
RACIAL/ETHNIC COMPOSITION OF STUDENT BODY	11	29-30/
ATHLETIC PROGRAM	12	31-32/
GANGS	13	33-34/
DRUGS OR ALCOHOL PROBLEMS	14	35-36/
MORAL STANDARDS/DRESS CODE	15	37-38/
OTHER, (SPECIFY): _____	16	39-40/

12

OTHER RELATIVES

B19. And now I have a few questions about your relatives who do not live with you now.

Do you have any children who do not currently live with you in your (house/apartment)?

(Circle One)

YES .... 1 ---> ASK B20-B21   41/
NO .... 2 ---> GO TO B22

B20. How many of your children currently live in your home country?

NONE 00

OR   42-43/

ENTER NUMBER
OF CHILDREN:

B21. How many of your children currently live in the U.S. but do not stay with you in your (house/apartment)?

NONE 00

OR   44-45/

ENTER NUMBER
OF CHILDREN:

B22. Do you have any brothers or sisters who do not currently live with you in your (house/apartment)?

(Circle One)

YES .... 1 --> ASK B23-B24   46/
NO .... 2 --> GO TO B25

B23. How many of your brothers or sisters currently live in your home country?

NONE 00

OR   47-48/

ENTER NUMBER OF
BROTHERS/SISTERS:

B24. How many of your brothers or sisters currently live in the U.S. but do not stay with you in your (house/apartment)?

NONE 00

OR   49-50/

ENTER NUMBER OF
BROTHERS/SISTERS:

CARD 05

13

B25. Do you have a parent who does not currently live with you in your (house/apartment)?

(Circle One)

YES .... 1 --> ASK B26   51/

NO .... 2 --> GO TO SECTION C, NEXT PAGE

B26. Where does your mother or father live now--is it in your home country, somewhere else in the U.S. or in some other country?

	(A) MOTHER LIVES IN:	(B) FATHER LIVES IN:
HOME COUNTRY	1 52/	1 53/
ELSEWHERE IN U.S............	2	2
OTHER COUNTRY	3	3
PARENT IS DECEASED........	4	4
PARENT LIVES WITH RESPONDENT	5	5

CARD 05

14

SECTION C: FAMILY'S USE OF HEALTH AND PUBLIC SERVICES

Now I have some questions about places where you and other members of your family go when you are sick or need medical advice. Please answer these questions about the members of your family who usually live with you in this (house/apartment).

C1. In the past 12 months, did anyone in your family who lives here, including yourself, get medical care from a (READ ITEM)?

		DID R OR FAMILY USE IN PAST 12 MONTHS?		
		YES	NO	
a.	Private physician or clinic?	1	2	54/
b.	Prepaid Health Plan or HMO (Health Maintenance Organization)--such as Kaiser, Cigna, or Healthnet?	1	2	55/
c.	County Public Hospital (including the emergency room)?	1	2	56/
d.	Some other kind of hospital (including the emergency room)?	1	2	57/
e.	County Health Clinic or Health Center?	1	2	58/
f.	Free Health Clinic or Health Center?	1	2	59/
g.	Family Planning Clinic or Program?	1	2	60/
h.	Prenatal Care Clinic or Program?	1	2	61/
i.	Other Child Health Services or Program (for example, a well child care program)?	1	2	62/
j.	Private Dentist?	1	2	63/
k.	Public Dental Clinic?	1	2	64/
l.	Tuberculosis Control Program (TB)?	1	2	65/
m.	Communicable Disease Program (for example, hepatitis)?	1	2	66/
n.	Immunization Program or Services (for example, measles, tetanus)?	1	2	67/
o.	Venereal Disease or VD Program (that is, a sexually-transmitted disease or STD program, for gonnorhea, syphilis)?	1	2	68/
p.	Rape Crisis Center?	1	2	69/
q.	Another type of place?	1	2	70/

➡ What is the name of this program? _____

71-72/

CARD 05

15

CARD 06

7-8/
1-6/

C6. Who pays for this health insurance--was it obtained from...(READ LIST):

(Circle All That Apply)

Your current employer or union, ... 1 13/

Your (husband/wife)'s current employer or union, ... 2 14/

Some other relative's current employer or union, ... 3 15/

Or, was it privately purchased by you or someone else in your family? 4 16/

C7. Are any other members of your family covered by this health insurance policy? IF YES: Who is covered?

(Circle All That Apply)

NO OTHER FAMILY MEMBERS COVERED BY POLICY . 1 17/

SPOUSE 2 18/

CHILD OR CHILDREN WHO LIVE IN HOUSEHOLD 3 19/

CHILD OR CHILDREN WHO DO NOT LIVE IN HOUSEHOLD 4 20/

SOMEONE ELSE (Who?) _____ 5 21/
RELATIONSHIP TO RESPONDENT

CARD 06

C2. Are you or anyone else in your family who lives here, currently covered by a government sponsored health policy such as MediCal, Medicaid, or the Child Health and Disability Program (CHDP)?

(Circle One)

YES 1   9/

NO 2

C3. Are you, yourself, covered by private health insurance, such as Aetna, Blue Cross, Prudential or some other type of private health insurance?

(Circle One)

YES 1   10/

NO 2

C4. Are you personally covered by a prepaid health plan or HMO (Health Maintenance Organization), such as Kaiser, Cigna, or Healthnet?

(Circle One)

YES .... 1 --> GO TO C6   11/

NO .... 2 --> ASK C5

C5. INTERVIEWER CHECK C3 AND C4:

DOES RESPONDENT HAVE PRIVATE HEALTH INSURANCE OR A PREPAID HEALTH PLAN (HMO)*

(Circle One)

YES .... 1 --> ASK C6   12/

NO .... 2 --> GO TO C8

16

C8. In the past 12 months, did anyone in your family who lives here, including yourself, get help from any of the following public services?
READ LIST.

PUBLIC SERVICES:	DID RESPONDENT OR FAMILY USE IN PAST 12 MONTHS?		
	YES	NO	
a. AFDC (Aid to Families With Dependent Children)?	1	2	22/
b. Food Stamps?	1	2	23/
c. WIC (Women, Infants, and Children Program)?	1	2	24/
d. School Breakfast or Lunch Programs (free or reduced price)?	1	2	25/
e. School Special Education Programs?	1	2	26/
f. Child Welfare or Protective Services?	1	2	27/
g. Women's or Family Shelters?	1	2	28/
h. Programs to Help Families Pay Their Utility Bills (gas, telephone, electricity, water)?	1	2	29/
i. Programs to Help Families Pay Their Rent (rent payments or subsidies)?	1	2	30/
j. Programs That Provide Food or Lodging for Families?	1	2	31/
k. Senior Citizen Programs and Services (meals, household chores, day care)?	1	2	32/
l. Counseling Programs and Services (alcoholism and drug abuse, violence, mental health)?	1	2	33/
m. Legal Services?	1	2	34/
n. Public Libraries (information and referral programs and services, help with translation)?	1	2	35/
o. Public Transportation System (public buses, RTD, CALTRANS, DIAL-A-RIDE)?	1	2	36/
p. Recreational and Park Services (public swimming pool, recreation center, park)?	1	2	37/
q. Unemployment Compensation?	1	2	38/
r. Worker's Compensation?	1	2	39/
s. General Relief Programs (this is an emergency relief program that provides special funds for food, shelter, or clothing)?	1	2	40/
t. Programs to Help You Find a Job (public employment agency or job training programs)?	1	2	41/

CARD 06

17

CARD 06

I'd like to get your opinions about the types of programs and services that you think (Filipinos/Salvadoreans/Central Americans) in your community currently need in order to adjust to living and working in the Los Angeles area.

C9. Could you tell me what you think is the most important public program or service that is needed to help (Filipinos/ Salvadoreans/Central Americans) n your community? PROBE: What else? RECORD VERBATIM.

42-43/ _____

44-45/ _____

46-47/ _____

_____

_____

_____

_____

_____

_____

_____

_____

_____

_____

_____

18

SECTION D: MIGRATION ATTITUDES, MENTAL HEALTH AND STRESS

Now I have some questions about how you felt when you first came to the U.S. and how you feel about living here.

D1. Did you have any problems with any of the following things when you first came to the United States: (READ LIST)

(Circle One Number On Each Line)

		YES	NO	
a.	getting a job?	1	2	48/
b.	finding somewhere to live?	1	2	49/
c.	English language?	1	2	50/
d.	American customs?	1	2	51/
e.	loneliness?	1	2	52/
f.	lack of friends?	1	2	53/
g.	homesickness?	1	2	54/
h.	something else?	1	2	55/
	What? _____			

D2. How satisfied are you now with life in the U.S.? Are you completely satisfied, very satisfied, fairly satisfied, a little dissatisfied, or very dissatisfied?

(Circle One)

COMPLETELY SATISFIED	1	56/
VERY SATISFIED	2	
FAIRLY SATISFIED	3	
A LITTLE DISSATISFIED	4	
VERY DISSATISFIED	5	

And now I have some questions about how you've been feeling in the past 30 days.

D3. In the past 30 days, how often have you felt nervous and "stressed"? Was it: (READ LIST)

(Circle One)

Very often,	1	57/
Fairly often,	2	
Sometimes,	3	
Almost never, or	4	
Never?	5	

D4. In the past 30 days, how often have you felt confident about your ability to handle your personal problems? Was it: (READ LIST)

(Circle One)

Very often,	1	58/
Fairly often,	2	
Sometimes,	3	
Almost never, or	4	
Never?	5	

CARD 06

19

CARD 06

20

D5. In the past 30 days, how often have you felt that things were going your way? Was it: (READ LIST)

(Circle One)

59/

Very often,	1
Fairly often,	2
Sometimes,	3
Almost never, or	4
Never?	5

D6. In the past 30 days, how often have you felt difficulties were piling up so high that you could not overcome them? Was it: (READ LIST)

(Circle One)

60/

Very often,	1
Fairly often,	2
Sometimes,	3
Almost never, or	4
Never?	5

SECTION E: WORK HISTORY

I'd like to ask you a few questions about work you may have done recently.

E1. What were you doing most of last week--working, keeping house, going to school or something else?

(Circle One)

WORKING	1	--> GO TO E4
WITH A JOB BUT NOT AT WORK	2	
LOOKING FOR WORK	3	
KEEPING HOUSE	4	
GOING TO SCHOOL	5	ASK E2
UNABLE TO WORK	6	
Why? RETIRED	7	
OTHER (SPECIFY)	8	

61/

62–63/

E2. Did you do any work at all last week not counting housework?

(Circle One)

YES 1
NO 2

64/

E3. INTERVIEWER CHECK: E1 AND E2

DID R WORK LAST WEEK?

(Circle One)

YES .... 1 --> ASK E4
NO .... 2 --> GO TO E24, PAGE 24

65/

E4. Were you working at one job or more than one job last week?

(Circle One)

ONE .... 1 --> GO TO E6
MORE THAN ONE ... 2 --> ASK E5

66/

E5. Since you're working at more than one job, I'd like to talk to you about your main job--where you worked the most hours.

MAIN JOB OR ONLY JOB

E6. Could you tell me what kind of work you were doing last week (on your main job)?

RECORD VERBATIM

_____

67/

_____

68–70/

_____

71–73/

CARD 06

21

CARD 07

7-8/
1-6/

MAIN JOB OR ONLY JOB

E7. What were your most important duties at (this job/your main job)?

RECORD VERBATIM

_____ 9/

E8. Were you self-employed or working for someone else at your (main) job?

(Circle One)

SELF EMPLOYED .... 1 --> GO TO E10   10/

WORKING FOR SOMEONE ELSE .... 2 --> ASK E9

E9. Who did you work for? (RECORD NAME OF COMPANY, BUSINESS, ORGANIZATION OR OTHER EMPLOYER.)

RECORD VERBATIM

_____ 11/

E10. What kind of business or industry is this?

RECORD VERBATIM

_____ 12/

E11. When did you begin working at (this job/your main job)?

☐☐ / ☐☐   13-16/
MONTH   YEAR

E12. How many hours do you *usually* work per week at (this job/your main job)?

HOURS PER WEEK: ☐☐   17-18/

E13. How are you *usually* paid on this job? Is that by the hour, day, week or some other way?

(Circle One)   19/

PIECE 1

HOUR 2

DAY 3

WEEKLY 4

EVERY TWO WEEKS 5

TWICE A MONTH 6

MONTHLY 7

OTHER (SPECIFY): 8

_____

E14. How much per week do you *usually* earn at this job, *before* deductions? Include any overtime pay, commissions, or tips usually received.

DOLLARS PER WEEK: $ ☐☐☐   20-23/

E15. Are deductions *usually* taken out of your pay?

(Circle One)   24/

YES .... 1 --> ASK E16

NO............ 2 --> GO TO E17

CARD 07

22

MAIN JOB OR ONLY JOB

E16. Which of the following deductions are usually taken out of your pay? (READ LIST)

(Circle One Number On Each Line)

	YES	NO	DON'T KNOW	
a. State taxes?	1	2	3	25/
b. Federal taxes?	1	2	3	26/
c. Social security deductions?	1	2	3	27/
d. Health insurance deductions?	1	2	3	28/

E17. How did you find this job?

_____

(Circle One)

CHECKED WITH PUBLIC EMPLOYMENT AGENCY 1   29/
CHECKED WITH PRIVATE EMPLOYMENT AGENCY 2
CHECKED WITH EMPLOYER DIRECTLY 3
CHECKED WITH FRIENDS OR RELATIVES 4
PLACED OR ANSWERED ADS 5
DAYWORK--WAITED FOR PICKUP 6
OTHER (SPECIFY): _____ 7

E18. In your workplace, are the people you work with mostly (Filipino/Salvadorean/Central American), a mix of nationalities, or are they mostly some other nationality?

(Circle One)

MOSTLY FILIPINOS/SALVADOREANS/
CENTRAL AMERICANS 1   30/
MIX OF NATIONALITIES 2
MOSTLY SOME OTHER NATIONALITY 3
DOES NOT APPLY, WORK ALONE OR AT HOME 4

E19. In your workplace, are any of your co-workers or employees related to you?

(Circle One)

YES .... 1 --> How many? _____ 31/
                                                        32-33/
NO 2

E20. INTERVIEWER CHECK E4, PAGE 21:

IS R WORKING AT ONE JOB OR MORE THAN ONE JOB NOW?

(Circle One)

ONE JOB .... 1 --> GO TO E31, PAGE 26   34/
MORE THAN ONE JOB .. 2 --> ASK E21

22a

CARD 07

CARD 07

ASK IF RESPONDENT HAS MORE THAN ONE JOB NOW

E21. How many jobs do you have now besides your main job?

(Circle One)

ONE 1   35/

TWO 2

THREE OR MORE 3

E22. How many hours per week do you usually work at (this other job/these other jobs)?

HOURS PER WEEK: ☐☐   36–37/

E23. How much do you usually earn per week at (this job/these jobs), before deductions? Include any overtime pay, commissions, or tips usually received.

DOLLARS PER WEEK: $ ☐☐☐☐   38–41/

GO TO E31, PAGE 26 →

23

```
┌─────────────────────────────────────────────────┐
│  ASK THESE QUESTIONS  IF RESPONDENT IS NOT EMPLOYED NOW  │
└─────────────────────────────────────────────────┘
```

E24. Have you been looking for work during the past 4 weeks?

(Circle One)

YES................ 1   --> ASK E25   42/

NO.................. 2   --> GO TO E27

E25. What have you been doing in the past 4 weeks to find work?

PROBE: Anything else?

_____

_____

(Circle All That Apply)

CHECKED WITH PUBLIC EMPLOYMENT AGENCY........ 1   43/

CHECKED WITH PRIVATE EMPLOYMENT AGENCY 2   44/

CHECKED WITH EMPLOYER DIRECTLY 3   45/

CHECKED WITH FRIENDS OR RELATIVES 4   46/

PLACED OR ANSWERED ADS....................... 5   47/

WAITED FOR DAYWORK PICKUP.................... 6   48/

NOTHING...................................... 7   49/

OTHER (SPECIFY): 8   50/

E26. How many weeks have you been looking for work?

NUMBER OF WEEKS: ☐☐   51–52/

24

E27. Are you collecting unemployment compensation now?

(Circle One)

YES................ 1   53/

NO................. 2

E28. Since you came to the U.S., have you ever worked for pay?

(Circle One)

YES................ 1   --> GO TO E30   54/

NO................. 2   --> ASK E29

E29. Where were you living when you first came to the U.S.--was it in Los Angeles, some other city in California, or some other place?

(Circle One)

LOS ANGELES................ 1   55/

ELSEWHERE IN CALIFORNIA.... 2 } GO TO E39, PAGE 28

OTHER PLACE................ 3

Where? _____ STATE   56–57/

CARD 07

CARD 07

ASK E30 IF RESPONDENT IS NOT EMPLOYED NOW

E30. The next few questions are about the last job you had in the U.S.

A. What was your last job? Could you tell me what kind of work you were doing at that time?

_____ 58-60/

_____ 61-63/

B. When did you begin that job?

☐☐ / ☐☐ 64-67/
MONTH   YEAR

C. When did you leave that job?

☐☐ / ☐☐ 68-71/
MONTH   YEAR

D. How many hours per week did you usually work at that job?

☐☐ 72-73/
HOURS PER WEEK:

E. How much did you usually earn per week at that job before deductions? Include any overtime pay, commissions, or tips usually received.

DOLLARS PER WEEK: $ ☐☐☐☐ 74-77/

25

CARD 08 7-8/
1-6/

FIRST JOB IN U.S.

E31. Now I'd like to ask you about your first job in the U.S. When did that job start?

```
┌──┬──┐ / ┌──┬──┐
└──┴──┘   └──┴──┘
 MONTH     YEAR
```
9-12/

E32. What was your first job in the U.S.? Could you tell me what kind of work you were doing at that time?
RECORD VERBATIM

_____ 13-15/

_____ 16-18/

E33. Are you still working at that job?

(Circle One)

YES............ 1 --> GO TO E39
NO............. 2 --> ASK E34

19/

E34. How long did you work at that job?

LENGTH: _____ 20-21/

CODE PERIOD: (Circle One)

DAYS......... 1
WEEKS....... 2
MONTHS...... 3
YEARS....... 4

22/

E35. Were you working at one job or more than one job at that time?

(Circle One)

ONE................... 1
MORE THAN ONE 2

23/

E36. How many hours per week did you usually work at (this job/all the jobs) you had at that time?

HOURS WORKED: ☐☐ 24-25/

E37. How much money did you usually earn per week before deductions at (the job/all jobs) you had at that time? Include any overtime pay, commissions, or tips usually received.

DOLLARS PER WEEK: $ ☐☐☐ 26-29/

E38. Where were you living when you got your first job in the U.S.--was it in Los Angeles, some other city in California, or some other place?

(Circle One)

LOS ANGELES.............. 1
ELSEWHERE IN CALIFORNIA.. 2
OTHER PLACE.............. 3
    Where? _____ STATE

30/

31-32/

E39. Since you came to the U.S., have you ever had trouble finding a job or keeping a job because you could not prove you were living here legally?

(Circle One)

YES......... 1
NO.......... 2

33/

CARD 08

26

LAST JOB IN HOME COUNTRY

E40. We're interested in learning more about the kinds of jobs people had before they came to the U.S. Did you ever work in (COUNTRY OF ORIGIN)?

(Circle One)

YES......... 1 --> ASK E41   34/

NO........... 2 --> GO TO SECTION F, PAGE 29

E41. Think about the last job you had before you came to the U.S. What kind of work were you doing at that time? If you had more than one job, please tell me about your main job at that time.

PROBE: What were your main activities or duties?

_____   35-37/

_____   38-40/

_____

E42. When did you begin that job?

☐☐ / ☐☐   41-44/
MONTH   YEAR

E43. When did you leave that job?

☐☐ / ☐☐   45-48/
MONTH   YEAR

E44. Were you self-employed or working for someone else at that time?

(Circle One)

SELF-EMPLOYED............. 1   49/

WORKING FOR SOMEONE ELSE.... 2

E45. Were you working at one job or more than one job at that time?

(Circle One)

ONE JOB................. 1   50/

MORE THAN ONE JOB........ 2

E46. How many hours per week did you usually work at (this job/all these jobs) at that time?

HOURS PER WEEK: ☐☐   51-52/

CARD 08

27

CARD 08

E47. How much did you usually earn per week (at this job/all these
jobs) before deductions? Include any overtime pay,
commissions, or tips usually received.

AMOUNT PER WEEK:

53-59/

➡ CODE CURRENCY: (Circle One)

DOLLARS (US) 1

COLONE (EL SALVADOR) 2

PESO (PHILIPPINES) 3

OTHER (SPECIFY) 4

60/

28

SECTION F: MIGRATION HISTORY AND STATUS

F1.   Is this the first time you have lived in the U.S.?

(Circle One)

YES.................. 1   --> GO TO F5

NO.................. 2   --> ASK F2   61/

F2.   When was your first visit to the U.S. for three months or longer?

☐☐ / ☐☐
MONTH   YEAR   62–65/

F3.   How long did you stay in the U.S. that time?

_____ YEARS   66–67/

AND/OR

_____ MONTHS   68–69/

F4.   Which of the categories on this card best describes your status when you came to the U.S. in (DATE IN F2)?

SHOW CARD #1.

(Circle One)

PERMANENT RESIDENT 01

TEMPORARY RESIDENT 02

WITHOUT PAPERS 03

TEMPORARY WORK VISA 04

STUDENT VISA 05

TOURIST VISA 06

DEPENDENT ON SOMEONE ELSE'S VISA
(FOR EXAMPLE, YOUR HUSBAND/WIFE,
PARENT OR GUARDIAN) 07

EXPIRED VISA 08

ASYLEE 09

TEMPORARY PROTECTED IMMIGRANT (TPS)... 10

SOME OTHER PAPER? 11

What? _____

70–71/

CARD 08

29

F5. When did you come to the U.S. (this time)?

[ ][ ] / [ ][ ]
MONTH   YEAR

72-75/

F6. SHOW CARD #1. Please tell me the number for the category that describes your status when you came to the U.S. in (DATE in F5).

(Circle One)

76-77/

PERMANENT RESIDENT	01
TEMPORARY RESIDENT	02
WITHOUT PAPERS	03
TEMPORARY WORK VISA	04
STUDENT VISA	05
TOURIST VISA	06
DEPENDENT ON SOMEONE ELSE'S VISA (FOR EXAMPLE, YOUR HUSBAND/WIFE, PARENT OR GUARDIAN)	07
EXPIRED VISA	08
ASYLEE	09
TEMPORARY PROTECTED IMMIGRANT (TPS)	10
SOME OTHER PAPER?	11

What? _____

F7. SHOW CARD #2. What category on this card best describes the main reason you came to the United States (this time)?

(Circle One)

78-79/

TO FIND WORK OR A BETTER JOB	01
TO REUNITE FAMILY	02
TO GET A BETTER EDUCATION	03
TO GET A BETTER LIFE AND MORE OPPORTUNITY	04
FLED FROM POLITICAL PERSECUTION	05
FLED FROM RELIGIOUS PERSECUTION	06
FEARED FOR OWN LIFE	07
FEARED FOR FAMILY MEMBERS' LIVES	08
OTHER REASON (SPECIFY) _____	09

CARD 08

30

F8. Are you a naturalized U.S. citizen?

(Circle One)

YES .... 1 --> ASK F9
NO .... 2 --> GO TO F10

9/

F9. In what year did you become a citizen?

YEAR: 19 [ ] --> GO TO SECTION G, PAGE 34

10–11/

F10. Do you plan to become a U.S. citizen in the next five years?

(Circle One)

YES 1
NO 2
DON'T KNOW/UNSURE 3

12/

CARD 09 7–8/
1–6/

F11. SHOW CARD #1. Please tell me the number for the category that describes your current status.

(Circle One)

PERMANENT RESIDENT .... 01 ⎱ GO TO F14
TEMPORARY RESIDENT .... 02 ⎰
WITHOUT PAPERS .... 03 --> GO TO F13
TEMPORARY WORK VISA 04
STUDENT VISA 05
TOURIST VISA 06
DEPENDENT ON SOMEONE ELSE'S VISA (FOR EXAMPLE, YOUR HUSBAND/WIFE, PARENT OR GUARDIAN) .... 07 ASK F12
EXPIRED VISA 08
ASYLEE 09
TEMPORARY PROTECTED IMMIGRANT (TPS) 10
SOME OTHER PAPER? 11
What? _____

13–14/

F12. When (does/did) your visa or permit expire?

[ ] / [ ]
MONTH   YEAR

15–18/

CARD 09

31

F13. Do you think you will change to a resident status in the next 12 months?

(Circle One)

YES.......................... 1   19/
NO............................ 2

F14. Did you apply for the SAW or IRCA amnesty programs that began in 1986? (SAW stands for "Special Agricultural Worker's Permit" and IRCA stands for the Immigration Reform and Control Act.) IF YES, PROBE: Which program did you apply for?

(Circle One)

YES, APPLIED FOR SAW.. 1   --> GO TO F16   20/
YES, APPLIED FOR IRCA... 2   --> GO TO F16
NO............................. 3   --> ASK F15

F15. Why didn't you apply for these amnesty programs?

PROBE: Any other reason?

_____
_____
_____

(Circle All That Apply)

HAD NOT LIVED HERE LONG ENOUGH TO QUALIFY.... 1   21/
COULD NOT PROVE ELIGIBILITY 2   22/
DIDN'T KNOW WHERE TO GO TO APPLY 3   23/
DIDN'T KNOW ABOUT THE PROGRAM 4   24/
AFRAID TO APPLY 5   25/
OTHER 6   26/
_____   27-28/
                                    29-30/

32

F16. In your opinion, has the amnesty program affected your ability to obtain work, the types of jobs you can get or the pay you can earn?

(Circle One)

YES 1   --> ASK F17   31/
NO............................. 2   --> GO TO F18

F17. How has the amnesty program affected you personally?

RECORD VERBATIM

Probe: Anything else?

_____   32-33/
_____   34-35/
_____   36-37/
_____
_____
_____

CARD 09

CARD 09

F18. INTERVIEWER, CHECK F11:

WHAT IS RESPONDENT'S CURRENT IMMIGRATION STATUS?

(Circle One)

PERMANENT RESIDENT.......... 1   GO TO SECTION G,

TEMPORARY RESIDENT 2   NEXT PAGE

TEMPORARY PROTECTED
IMMIGRANT (TPS)............. 3

OTHER VISA OR PERMIT 4

WITHOUT PAPERS 5   ASK F19

DON'T KNOW 6

38/

F19. Did you apply for the special temporary protected immigrant status program (TPS) that began in 1990?

(Circle One)

YES.................. 1 --> GO TO SECTION G

NO................... 2 --> ASK F20

39/

F20. Do you think you will apply for the special temporary protected immigrant status (TPS) program in the next year?

(Circle One)

YES............. 1

NO............. 2

40/

33

CARD 10

7-8/
1-6/

SECTION G: FAMILY HOUSING, EXPENSES, INCOME, AND TAXES

Now, I have a few questions about your family's housing and major expenses.

G1. Does your family rent or own this (house/apartment)?

(Circle One)

RENT........................ 1 --> GO TO G4

OWN......................... 2 --> ASK G2-G3

9/

G2. In what year did your family purchase your home?

[ ][ ] 19

10-11/

G3. When your family bought your house in (YEAR), how much did you pay for it?

$ [ ][ ][ ][ ][ ][ ]
PURCHASE PRICE

12-17/

G4. Next, I'd like to ask you about your family's expenses in the past 30 days. Including yourself, how much money did your family spend on each of the following things in the past 30 days? (READ LIST) (Just your best estimate)

FAMILY EXPENSES:

ROUND TO NEAREST
$ SPENT

a. rent or house payments? .... $ _____ 18-21/

b. payments for utilities like gas, electricity, or water? .... $ _____ 22-25/

c. telephone bills? .... $ _____ 26-29/

d. gas for your car(s)? .... $ _____ 30-33/

e. other car expenses like registration, smog inspection, or drivers' license? .... $ _____ 34-37/

f. groceries including food stamps, but not counting beer, wine and other alcohol? .... $ _____ 38-41/

g. beer, wine, and other alcohol? .... $ _____ 42-45/

h. cigarettes, cigars, or tobacco? .... $ _____ 46-49/

i. food from restaurants, fast food places, etc.? .... $ _____ 50-53/

j. entertainment, for example, going to movies, sports events, or other things your family does for fun or relaxation? .... $ _____ 54-57/

k. education or job training expenses? .... $ _____ 58-61/

CARD 10

34

G5. Between January and December of 1990, did anyone in your family who lives here, including yourself, send any money to relatives in your home country?

(Circle One)

YES................ 1 -> ASK G6   62/
NO................. 2 -> GO TO G8

G6. For all of 1990, approximately how much money did you or other members of your family send to relatives in your home country? (Just your best estimate)

63-67/

$ [ ][ ][ ][ ][ ]

OR

DON'T KNOW....... 8 -> ASK G7   68/
REFUSED.......... 9 -> ASK G7

G7. Could you tell me which of the following categories comes closest to the amount of money your family sent to relatives in your home country during 1990? (READ LIST) Would you say:

(Circle One)

Less than $100,....................... 1   69/
Between $101 and $500,................ 2
Between $501 and $1000,............... 3
Between $1001 and $5000,.............. 4
Between $5001 and $10,000, or...... 5
More than $10,000..................... 6

G8. During 1990, did you or anyone in your family who lives here receive any money from friends or relatives who do not usually live in this (house/apartment)?

(Circle One)

YES................ 1 -> ASK G9   70/
NO................. 2 -> GO TO G11

G9. In 1990, how much money did you and your family receive from friends or relatives who do not live in this (house/apartment)? (Just your best estimate)

71-75/

$ [ ][ ][ ][ ][ ]

OR

DON'T KNOW....... 8 -> ASK G10   76/
REFUSED.......... 9 -> ASK G10

G10. Which of the following categories comes closest to that amount? Was it: (READ LIST)

(Circle One)

Less than $100,....................... 1   77/
Between $101 and $500,................ 2
Between $501 and $1000,............... 3
Between $1001 and $5000,.............. 4
Between $5001 and $10,000, or...... 5
More than $10,000..................... 6

CARD 10

35

G11. Now I'd like to ask you a question about your family's income during 1990. _Including yourself_, how much money did the people in your family who live here now receive from wages, pensions, real estate or any other source during 1990? Please include _all_ sources of income before taxes for _all_ members of your family who are living here now. (Just your best estimate)

9-14/

ENTER DOLLAR AMOUNT: $ ☐☐☐☐☐☐ --> GO TO G13

OR

15/

DON'T KNOW .... 8 --> ASK G12

REFUSED .... 9 --> ASK G12

CARD 11 7-8/
         1-6/

G12. SHOW CARD #3. Could you tell me which of the categories on this card comes closest to your family's total income for all of 1990?

(Circle One)

16-17/

A. LESS THAN $7,500 01
B. $7,500 - $9,999 02
C. $10,000 - $12,499 03
D. $12,500 - $14,999 04
E. $15,000 - $19,999 05
F. $20,000 - $29,999 06
G. $30,000 - $42,499 07
H. $42,500 - 57,499 08
I. $57,500 - $69,999 09
J. $70,000 OR MORE 10
K. REFUSED 11
L. DON'T KNOW 12

CARD 11

36

G13. Did you (or your husband/wife) file a federal income tax form for last year--that is, 1990?

(Circle One)

YES............................. 1 --> ASK G14   18/

NO.............................. 2 --> GO TO G15

G14. Approximately, how much did you (and your husband/wife) pay in federal income taxes last year (1990)? Please include the amount that was taken from your paychecks and any additional federal taxes that you paid at the end of the year. (Just your best estimate)

$ [ ][ ][ ][ ][ ]   --> GO TO G16   19-23/

OR

DON'T KNOW .... 8 } GO TO G16   24/

REFUSED .... 9 }

G15. What was the main reason you (and your husband/wife) didn't file a federal tax return last year (1990)?

RECORD VERBATIM:

_____   25-26/

_____   27-28/

_____   29-30/

_____

_____

G16. That's the end of this interview. I just need to ask a few last questions for our record keeping.

G17. Do you have a telephone at this (house/apartment)?

(Circle One)

YES.............................. 1 --> ASK G18   31/

NO............................... 2 --> GO TO G19

G18. Just in case my office wants to make sure I was here to do this interview, could you tell me your telephone number? RECORD # ON RECORD FOLDER.

(Circle One)

PHONE # RECORDED ON FOLDER............ 1   32/

PHONE # REFUSED........................ 2

COMMENTS:

_____

G19. Thank you very much for your time. We really appreciate your help with this important study.

BEFORE LEAVING, GIVE RESPONDENT HIS/HER GROCERY CERTIFICATE AND THANK YOU CARD.

G20. INTERVIEWER, RECORD

TIME ENDED: [ ][ ] : [ ][ ]   33-36/

AM........ 1   37/

PM........ 2

INTERVIEWER COMPLETE ITEMS ON NEXT PAGE IMMEDIATELY AFTER LEAVING

CARD 11

37

SECTION H: INTERVIEWER REMARKS

INTERVIEWER: COMPLETE THESE REMARKS AS SOON AS
YOU HAVE FINISHED THE QUESTIONNAIRE.

H1.   IN GENERAL, WHAT WAS THE RESPONDENT'S ATTITUDE
TOWARD THE INTERVIEW?

(Circle One)   38/

FRIENDLY AND INTERESTED 1

COOPERATIVE BUT NOT PARTICULARLY
INTERESTED 2

IMPATIENT AND RESTLESS 3

HOSTILE 4

H2.   IN GENERAL, WAS THE RESPONDENT'S
UNDERSTANDING OF THE QUESTIONS.

(Circle One)   39/

GOOD 1

FAIR 2

POOR? 3

H3.   LIST QUESTIONS THAT CONFUSED, ANGERED, OR
CAUSED DISCOMFORT TO THE RESPONDENT OR
QUESTIONS THAT YOU FEEL THE RESPONDENT DID NOT
ANSWER TRUTHFULLY. *EXPLAIN*

NONE 1   40/

OR

SECTION	QUESTION
_____ 41/	_____ 42–44/
_____ 45/	_____ 46–48/
_____ 49/	_____ 50–52/
_____ 53/	_____ 54–56/
_____ 57/	_____ 58–60/

DESCRIBE PROBLEM: _____

_____ 61–62/

_____ 63–64/

_____ 65–66/

_____ 67–68/

_____ 69–70/

CARD 11

38

CARD 12   7-8/
1-6/

H5. OTHER PERSONS PRESENT AT INTERVIEW WERE:

(Circle All That Apply)

NONE	1	40/
CHILDREN UNDER 6	2	41/
OLDER CHILDREN	3	42/
SPOUSE	4	43/
OTHER RELATIVES	5	44/
OTHER ADULTS	6	45/

H6. ANY OTHER COMMENTS ABOUT THIS INTERVIEW:

(Circle One)

YES 1   46/
NO 2

EXPLAIN:
_____ 47-48/
_____ 49-50/
_____ 51-52/

CARD 12

H4. LIST QUESTIONS WITH SKIP ERRORS, QUESTIONS THAT WERE CONFUSING TO YOU OR QUESTIONS THAT OTHERWISE DIDN'T WORK. EXPLAIN

NONE 1   9/

OR

SECTION		QUESTION	
____	10/	____	11-13/
____	14/	____	15-17/
____	18/	____	19-21/
____	22/	____	23-25/
____	26/	____	27-29/

DESCRIBE PROBLEM:
_____ 30-31/
_____ 32-33/
_____ 34-35/
_____ 36-37/
_____ 38-39/

39

CARD 12

REFUSAL/BREAKOFF/OTHER NON-INTERVIEW REPORT FORM

INTERVIEWER, RECORD IMMEDIATELY AFTER LEAVING RESPONDENT

1. Reason for non-interview:

(Circle One)

Refusal	01	} CONTINUE WITH Q.2
Break-off	02	
Respondent incapable (Explain Below)	03	
Language Barrier (Explain Below)	04	
Secure residence (Explain Below)	05	
Security apartment building (Explain Below)	06	} RECORD OTHER COMMENTS BELOW
Manager refused entry to building (Explain Below)	07	
Vacant building	08	
Business	09	
Other (Explain Below)	10	

53-54/

1A. Other comments on this case?

_____

_____

_____

_____

55/

40

FOR REFUSALS AND BREAK-OFFS: Q.2 - Q.14

2. What was the reason given for the refusal/breakoff?

(Circle All That Apply)

No reason given	1	56/
Too confidential/personal	2	57/
Too busy/not interested	3	58/
Negative reaction to study	4	59/
Negative reaction to surveys in general	5	60/
Does not think legitimate/mistrusts interviewer	6	61/
Interview sounds too long/Is taking too long	7	62/
Too ill	8	63/
Other reason	9	64/
What? _____		

3. Exactly what did the respondent say when he/she refused or broke-off the interview?
   (RECORD EXACT WORDS - TRANSLATE INTO ENGLISH IF RESPONDENT USED ANOTHER LANGUAGE):

65/

_____

_____

_____

_____

_____

_____

_____

CARD 12

41

CARD 12

4. What did you say or do to try to persuade the respondent to participate?

_____

_____

_____   66/

5. Did the respondent accept our flyer or any of our other materials?

                                         (Circle One)

     Yes 1
     No 2   67/

6. Respondent's Sex:
                                         (Circle One)

     Male.................1
     Female...............2   68/

7. Respondent's Age:
                                         (Circle One)

     Under 20 1
     20 - 29 2
     30 - 39 3
     40 - 49 4
     50 - 59 5
     Over 60................6
     Don't Know.............7   69/

8. Was the respondent the same person who completed the
    screener interviewr?
                                         (Circle One)

     Yes 1
     No 2
     Don't Know.........3   70/

42

CARD 12

9. WHO REFUSED:

(Circle One)

SELECTED RESPONDENT................................... 1
SPOUSE OF SELECTED RESPONDENT................ 2
SON OR DAUGHTER OF RESPONDENT.............. 3
PARENT OF RESPONDENT................................. 4
OTHER RELATIVE OF RESPONDENT.................. 5
NON-RELATED...(E.G., ROOMMATE, BOARDER).. 6
DON'T KNOW.. 7

71 /

10. TYPE OF STRUCTURE:

(Circle One)

SINGLE FAMILY HOUSE 1
MULTI-UNIT BUILDING/COMPLEX........... 2
MOBILE HOME 3
OTHER _____ 4
       What?

72 /

11. How strong was the refusal/break-off?

(Circle One)

Hostile 1
Firm, but not hostile........... 2
Mild, no hostility.............. 3

73 /

43

CARD 12

12. Do you think a different "type" of interviewer would be more successful at this residence?

(Circle One)

Yes 1   74/
No 2   75/

IF YES, EXPLAIN: _____

_____

13. At what point did the respondent refuse or break-off?

(Circle One)

Before you began introduction 1   76/
During introduction 2

OR

QUESTION NUMBER: [ ][ ]   77-79/

14. What is your recommendation for how we could complete the interview at this residence?

_____

_____

_____   80/

44

SHOW CARDS FOR MAIN INTERVIEW

CARD #1 -- ENGLISH (F4, F6, F11)

01   PERMANENT RESIDENT

02   TEMPORARY RESIDENT

03   WITHOUT PAPERS

04   TEMPORARY WORK VISA

05   STUDENT VISA

06   TOURIST VISA

07   DEPENDENT ON SOMEONE ELSE'S VISA
       (FOR EXAMPLE, YOUR HUSBAND/WIFE, PARENT OR GUARDIAN)

08   EXPIRED VISA

09   ASYLEE

10   TEMPORARY PROTECTED IMMIGRANT (TPS)

11   SOME OTHER PAPERS
       ⬇

       What? _____

CARD #2--ENGLISH (F7)

F7. Please tell me the number for the category
that best describes the <u>main</u> reason
you came to the United States (this time).

01   TO FIND WORK OR A BETTER JOB

02   TO REUNITE FAMILY

03   TO GET A BETTER EDUCATION

04   TO GET A BETTER LIFE AND MORE OPPORTUNITY

05   FLED FROM POLITICAL PERSECUTION

06   FLED FROM RELIGIOUS PERSECUTION

07   FEARED FOR OWN LIFE

08   FEARED FOR FAMILY MEMBERS' LIVES

09   OTHER REASON (SPECIFY)

_____

_____

CARD #3--ENGLISH (G13)

G13.   Could you tell me which of the categories on
this card comes closest to your household's total
income for all of 1990?

        A.   LESS THAN $7,500

        B. $7,500 - $9,999

        C. $10,000 - $12,449

        D. $12,500 - $14,999

        E. $15,000 - $19,999

        F. $20,000 - $29,999

        G. $30,000 - $42,499

        H. $42,500 - $57,499

        I. $57,500 - $69,999

        J. $70,000 OR MORE

INTERVIEWER REFERENCE CARD FOR C8

EXAMPLES OF PUBLIC PROGRAMS AND SERVICES

Alcohol and Drug Programs (C6ℓ)
MADD (213) 641-5017
National Clearing House for Alcohol and Drug Information (301) 468-2600
Charter Oak Hospital-Psychiatric Emergency Services (800) 654-2673
Manor West Hospital (213) 389-4181
Union Rescue Mission (213) 628-6103
Asian American Drug Abuse Program (213) 293-6284)
California Hispanic Commission on Alcohol and Drug Abuse, Inc. (213) 722-4529
El Centro Substance Abuse Treatment Center (213) 265-9228
Life Plus Foundation, Inc. (818) 769-3911
Via Avanta (818) 897-2609

Child Welfare and Protection Services (C6F)
John Rossi Youth Foundation (213) 393-0644
Options House (213) 467-8466
Teen Canteen (213) 463-8336
Big Brothers of Greater Los Angeles (213) 258-3333

Counselling - Mental Health (C6ℓ)
El Centro Community Mental Health Center (213) 725-1337
Community Counseling Service (213) 746-5260
Community Connection (213) 299-0961
Mental Health-Costal Asian/Pacific Mental Health Clinic (213) 217-7312

Employment Service Program (C6t)
E LA Occupation Center
PACE--Pacific Asian Consortium in Employment
CCAC--Central City Action Committee

Housing Assistance (C6i)
Ellis Hotel (213) 229-9663
US Mission/Hudson House (213) 465-0247
Home Loan Counseling Center (213) 224-8011 (213) 747-0807
Community Development Department (213) 485-3406

Job Training (C6t)
5 Employment Training Center: E LA
Employment Programs and Operations Section-JTPA Referral Service
Chicana Service Action Center

Legal Services (C6m)
Asian Pacific American Legal Center of Southern California (213) 748-2022
Legal Aid Foundation of Los Angeles (213) 252-3846 (Tape)
Public Defender (?13) 620-5402

Public Transportation (C6o)
Transport Department
CALTRANS
Souther California Rapid Transit
E LA Dial-A-Ride (213) 666-0895

Violence (C6ℓ)
CAB--Center Against Abusive Behavior (818) 796-7358
E LA Battered Women's Shelter (213) 268-7568 (800) 548-2722
Center for the Pacific Asian Family Center-Shelter (213) 653-4042
Haven House, Inc. (818) 564-8880

Women's Shelters (C6g)
Odyssey house
Woman's Building (213) 221-6161
Good Shepard Center for Homeless Women (213) 250-5241
E LA Battered Women's Shelter (213) 268-7568 (800) 548-2722

INTERVIEWER REFERENCE CARD FOR F4, F6, F11

| Examples of Non-Immigrant Visas |

A	=	Diplomate, Foreign
B	=	Visitors, Business, or Pleasure
E	=	Investment Traveler
F	=	Academic Student
G	=	Representative of International Agency
H	=	Temporary Worker
I	=	Journalist
J	=	Exchange Visits
K	=	Fiancé of U.S. Citizen
L	=	Inter-company
M	=	Non-Academic Student

| IMMIGRATION STATUS CODES AND LETTERS |

01 = PERMANENT RESIDENT (I130, I140)

02 = TEMPORARY RESIDENT

04 = TEMPORARY WORK VISA (H, I129H)

05 = STUDENT VISA (J, M, F, I20, P1, M1, J1)

06 = TOURIST VISA (B, I134, Affidavit of Support From Invité)

07 = DEPENDENT ON SOMEONE ELSE'S VISA

09 = ASYLEE (I589)

10 = TEMPORARY PROTECTED IMMIGRANT (TPS) (I817)

11 = SOME OTHER PAPERS (E-Visa, I126, K1 (Fiancé), I129F, L-Visa, I129L)

INFORMATION FLYERS

While you were out...

An interviewer from RAND came to your house to speak with you about the Los Angeles Community Survey.

We will come back again in the hope of finding someone at home.

Your household along with over 9,000 other households in the area, has been selected as part of a random sample of Los Angeles residents to participate in a short survey about how people adjust to life in Los Angeles.

The survey will only take about 5 minutes to complete.

RAND is a non-profit public policy research organization locate in Santa Monica, CA.

* We are not selling anything
* Our interviewers carry identification

If you have any questions about our work, please call RAND collect at:

(213) 393-0411, extension 6788 or 7288

———————————————
Interviewer Name   Date

Mientras Ud. estaba ausente...

Un entrevistador de la RAND vino a su casa a hablar con usted sobre la Encuesta de Comunidades de Los Angeles.

El entrevistador regresará esperando que usted lo reciba.

Su casa, junto con otras 9000 casas de esta área, ha sido seleccionada como parte de un estudio de los residentes de Los Angeles para participar en una encuesta de como se adapta la gente a la vida en Los Angeles.

La encuesta tomará solamente cinco minutos.

RAND es un centro de investigación que realiza estudios relacionados con la política pública, ubicado en Santa Mónica, Ca.

* No trataremos de venderle nada
* Nuestros entrevistadores llevarán credenciales

Si tiene cualquier pregunta sobre nuestro estudio, por favor llame por cobrar a RAND al:

(213) 393-0411, ext.6788 o 7288

———————————————
Nombre del entrevistador   Fecha

Samantalang wala kayo sa tahanan...

Isang tagapagtanong ng RAND ay nagpunta sa inyong tahanan para makipagusap sa inyo tungkol sa suriin ng komunidad ng Los Angeles.

Babalik ulit kami sa pag-asa na merong tao kaming masampitan sa inyong tahanan.

Ang inyong pamilya, kasama sa humigit-kumulang na 9000 mga pamilya na nakatira dito sa panig ng Los Angeles para sumali sa maiksing suriin upang malaman kung paano ang mga pamilyang ito ay nakakaangkop sa pamumunay dito sa Los Angeles.

Ang pagsusuri o pagtatanong na ito ay tatagal lamang ng limang minuto.

Ang RAND ay isang organisasyong pangmadlang, patakarang panaliksik (non-profit public-policy research organization) sa Santa Monica.

* Wala kaming ipinagbibili
* Ang aming mga tagapagtanong ay merong mga dalang identipikasyon

Kung merong kayong mga tanong tungkol sa aming trabaho, magtawag kayo ng "collect" sa RAND (213) 393-0411, extensiyon 6788 o 7288.

———————————————
Pangalan ng Tagapagtanong   Petsa

LOS ANGELES COMMUNITY SURVEY
QUESTIONS AND ANSWERS

FOR INFORMATION CALL:
(213) 393-0411, Ext. 6788 or 7288

For your convenience, a RAND supervisor is available to speak with you in: English, Spanish, or Tagalog

===

PURPOSE:
This is a survey of Los Angeles residents to learn more about how families from other countries adjust to living and working in Los Angeles.

This is a scientific research study and we are not part of any form of law enforcement. We are not selling anything. We have professional bilingual interviewers who carry a photo identification card.

WHO IS DOING THE STUDY?
The study is being carried out by RAND, which is a private, non-profit public policy research organization located in Santa Monica, California. RAND conducts research on many different topics such as health care, education and work training, housing for low income families, and many other topics of interest to members of the general public.

WHO IS SPONSORING THE STUDY?
This study is sponsored by a grant from the Ford Foundation. The Ford Foundation was incorporated in 1936 (by Henry Ford). Its purpose is to advance public well-being by identifying and contributing to the solution of problems of national and international importance. In addition to public policy research, the foundation also supports programs in the areas of human rights, education and culture, community service, and foreign affairs.

WHY WAS I SELECTED?
You were selected at random to participate in this important research study. We are asking a total of about 600 people who live in Los Angeles County to take part in this voluntary study.

WHY SHOULD I PARTICIPATE?
This is a chance to present your story as part of an unbiased, scientific research study that will provide an accurate picture of how foreign-born people adjust to life in Los Angeles and the special problems and needs that they have in making new lives in this area. By participating in this survey, you can make a valuable contribution to a study that may help plan future programs and services for members of your community.

WHAT ARE YOU ASKING ME TO DO?
We will ask you to complete an interview about you and your family's experiences living and working in Los Angeles. In about one month, an interviewer from RAND will contact you to schedule a convenient time to explain the survey and find out if you'd be willing to participate. That interview will take place some time this summer. We will ask you questions about your family, work, how and why you came to Los Angeles and what kinds of public services and programs you use.

YOU WILL GET:
A $5.00 gift certificate to use at your local grocery store if you decide to participate in the interview. This is a small token of our appreciation for your cooperation with this important research study.

===

MY NAME IS: _____ _____
                          RAND INTERVIEWER   TODAY'S DATE

I HOPE THAT YOU WILL BE ABLE TO PARTICIPATE IN THIS IMPORTANT STUDY!

MULTIVARIATE ANALYSES OF PUBLIC SERVICE USE

In this appendix we report results from multivariate analyses of the probabilities of using a variety of public services. The focus of the analyses is on the relationship between immigration status and public service use. We analyze whether the respondent or his or her family used any of the following public services in the past 12 months:

County clinic	Public hospital
Free clinic	Government-provided health insurance
WIC	Unemployment compensation
Public schools	School food program
Legal services	Public libraries
Public transportation	Parks

In Table E.1 we report the proportion of respondents using each of these services separately for each immigration status: with legal visa, without legal visa, resident, and citizen. In addition, we report the predicted probability of using each service by immigration status after controlling for a set of socioeconomic variables. The variables included as controls are country of origin, gender, age, education, whether ever attended school in the United States, ability to speak English, marital status, whether applied for amnesty under IRCA, and time since last migrated to the United States. All of this information is for the respondent in the household. In addition, the following household-level information was included in the analyses: household total monthly earnings, the number of adults in the household, and the number of children (age 18 or under) in the household.

In interpreting these results, the reader should keep in mind two serious limitations. The first is the relatively small sample size. A second limitation pertains to our measure of use of public services. We asked our survey respondents whether they or *anyone in their family* had used a specified service at least once over the past twelve months. But our measure of immigration status pertains to the respondent herself or himself, exclusive of other family members. The bias introduced by this difference in unit of observation is unknown.

The probability of use of each service was estimated by maximum-likelihood probit methods.[1] The predicted probability by immigration status was then obtained using the regression coefficients. If there were no statistically significant differences across immigration status groups, we did not report the predicted probabilities. If there were, we reported the predicted values in Table E.1. The predicted probabilities were evaluated at the following values of the control variables: a household in which the person interviewed was a male Salvadoran immigrant of average age (35.8 years), average years of schooling (9.8 years), who did not attend school in the United States, who speaks English well, has average monthly earnings ($259), has the average number of adults and children in the household, is married, did not apply under IRCA, and came to the United States at the time period of the average sample member (May 1981).

There are important differences in service use when the control variables are not included. Family members of citizens and residents are more likely to use public libraries and parks, and they are also more likely to have a child in public school. However, relative to families of undocumented and those with temporary legal visas, immigrants with permanent visas and citizens are less likely to use almost all other services. The first are more than twice as likely as family members of citizens to use public transportation, public hospitals, or school food programs. Family members of citizens, and to a lesser extent permanent residents, are much less likely to participate in government transfer programs such as food stamps or Women, Infants and Children.[2] While only 1 percent of citizens' family members participate in food stamps, approximately 20 percent of the undocumented or those with a temporary visa participate in either of these two programs.

When the socioeconomic variables are controlled statistically, significant differences in the use of services by immigrants and their family members across immigration status groups are found in only a few cases. Immigrants with a legal visa are statistically significantly more likely to use publicly provided legal services. While the predicted probability of using legal services is 20 percent for those with a temporary legal visa, only 6.1 percent of citizens are predicted to use such services. The only other public service that is used differentially by immigrants of different status is libraries. Immigrants who are citizens and their family members are more likely than all other immigrants to use public libraries.

In sum, the multivariate results imply that many of the differences in public service use across immigrant status groups are explained by socioeconomic differences. We found statistically significant differences in public service use for only three of the fourteen services examined. However, in several cases we did find substantively important differences across immigrant status groups in the multivariate analyses, but the estimates were imprecise. The imprecision of the estimates may be due to the small size of the sample.

---

[1] The full regression estimates are available from the authors upon request.

[2] The undocumented immigrants and most temporary visa holders are not themselves eligible for transfer programs.

Table E.1

Predicted Probability of Public Service Use by Immigration Status With and Without Controls

	Without Controls				With Controls			
Program	Undocumented	Temporary Legal Visa	Permanent Visa	Citizen	Undocumented	Temporary Legal Visa	Permanent Visa	Citizen
Child in school	14.9%	24.2%	30.5%	35.0%	No statistically significant differences[a]			
County clinic	24.8	24.2	11.9	5.1	No statistically significant differences[a]			
Public hospital	27.7	25.9	17.2	9.7	No statistically significant differences[a]			
Free clinic	9.9	9.8	6.1	3.4	No statistically significant differences[a]			
Government insurance	34.0	28.8	23.7	26.3	No statistically significant differences[a]			
Food stamps	19.8	16.8	10.6	0.6	No statistically significant differences[a]			
WIC	30.0	28.8	15.0	0.0	No statistically significant differences[a]			
School food	22.8	27.2	27.0	7.4	No statistically significant differences[a]			
Legal services	13.0	25.0	9.0	1.1	12.3	20.3	10.3	6.1
Public libraries	22.0	25.7	38.1	71.6	33.3	36.3	35.2	46.4
Public transportation	64.4	60.6	47.9	28.9	No statistically significant differences[a]			
Parks	53.5	44.7	59.0	70.5	No statistically significant differences[a]			
Unemployment compensation	8.0	9.2	10.4	8.0	No statistically significant differences[a]			
Observations	101	132[b]	245	177				

[a]If no statistically significant differences across immigration groups are found, then the predicted values are not estimated in the table. The predicted values are based on a male Salvadoran immigrant of average age (35.8 years), average years of schooling (9.8), who did not attend school in the United States, who speaks English well, has average monthly earnings ($259), has the average number of adults and children in the household, is married, did not apply under IRCA, and came to the United States at the average time period of the sample members (May 1981).

[b]Includes 88 respondents on Temporary Protective Status.

Berry, S., and D. Kanouse, "Physician Response to a Mailed Survey: An Experiment in Timing of Payment," *Public Opinion Quarterly*, Vol. 51, No. 1, 1987, pp. 102–114.

Comprehensive Adult Student Assessment System (CASAS), *A Survey of Newly Legalized Persons in California*, San Diego, CA, 1989.

Crane, Keith, Beth J. Asch, Joanna Zorn Heilbrunn, and Danielle C. Cullinane, *The Effect of Employer Sanctions on the Flow of Undocumented Immigrants to the United States*, Santa Monica, CA: RAND, JRI-03, 1990.

Fowler, Floyd J., *Survey Research Methods*, Newbury Park, CA: Sage Publications, Applied Social Research Methods Series, 1988.

Greenwell, Lisa, Julie DaVanzo, and R. Burciaga Valdez, *Social Ties, Wages, and Gender Among Salvadorean and Filipino Immigrants in Los Angeles*, Santa Monica, CA: RAND, DRU-213-PRIP, 1993.

Levine, Daniel B., Kenneth Hill, and Robert Warren (eds.), *Immigration Statistics: A Story of Neglect*, Panel on Immigration Statistics, Commission on Behavioral and Social Sciences and Education, National Research Council, Washington, D.C.: National Academy Press, 1985.

Marín, Gerardo, and VanOss Marín, Barbara, *Research with Hispanic Populations*, Newbury Park, CA: Sage Publications, Applied Social Research Methods Series, Vol. 23, 1991.

McDonnell, Lorraine M., and Paul T. Hill, *Newcomers in American Schools: Meeting the Educational Needs of Immigrant Youth*, Santa Monica, CA: RAND, MR-103-AWM/PRIP, 1993.

Portes, Alejandro, and Ruben G. Rumbaut, *Immigrant America: A Portrait*, Berkeley: University of California Press, 1990.

Rolph, Elizabeth S., *Immigration Policies: Legacy from the 1980s and Issues for the 1990s*, Santa Monica, CA: RAND, R-4184-FF, 1992.

Steeh, Charlotte G., "Trends in Nonresponse Rates, 1952–1979," *Public Opinion Quarterly*, Vol. 45, 1981, pp. 40–57.

Vernez, Georges, "Needed: A Federal Role in Helping Communities Cope with Immigration," in James B Steinberg, David W. Lyon, and Mary E. Vaiana, *Urban America: Policy Choices for Los Angeles and the Nation*, Santa Monica, CA: RAND, MR-100-RC, 1992.

————, *Statement of Georges Vernez Before the Select Committee on Statewide Immigration Impact*, California State Assembly, Santa Monica, CA: RAND, P-7853, 1993.

Vernez, Georges, and Kevin McCarthy, *Meeting the Economy's Labor Needs Through Immigration: Rationale and Challenges*, Santa Monica, CA: RAND, N-3052-FF, 1990.

Woodrow, Karen A., and Jeffrey S. Passel, "Post-IRCA Undocumented Immigration to the United States: An Assessment Based on the June 1988 CPS," in Frank D. Bean, Barry Edmonston, and Jeffrey S. Passel (eds.), *Undocumented Migration to the United States: IRCA and the Experience of the 1980s*, Washington, D.C.: The Urban Institute Press, 1990. Also published, Santa Monica, CA: RAND, JRI-07, 1990.

U.S. General Accounting Office (U.S. GAO), *Immigration: Data Not Sufficient for Proposed Legislation*, Report to the Chairman, Subcommittee on Immigration and Refugee Affairs, Committee on the Judiciary, U.S. Senate, GAO/PEMD-89-8, Gaithersburg, MD, December 28, 1988.